The Leicestershire & Rutland Village Book

Compiled by the Leicestershire & Rutland
Federation of Women's Institutes from notes
and illustrations sent by Institutes in the County

Published jointly by
Countryside Books, Newbury
and the LRFWI, Leicester

Countryside Books
3 Catherine Road
Newbury, Berkshire

ISBN 1 85306 056 9

Cover photograph of Bottesford
taken by Mrs S. M. Birley

Produced through MRM Associates Ltd, Reading
Typeset by Acorn Bookwork, Salisbury
Printed in England by J. W. Arrowsmith Ltd, Bristol

Foreword

Leicestershire and Rutland lie in the part of England known as the East Midlands. The Federation is predominantly rural, although the hosiery and allied trades of Leicester and the coalmining communities towards the South Derbyshire border have many examples of industrial archaeology. Charnwood Forest near Loughborough is the highest point, and much of the region is covered with rolling countryside providing peaceful valleys and pastures for agriculture. The market towns still reflect the importance of farming in spite of the other varied occupations of the twentieth century.

Rutland Water near Oakham is a recent addition. It covers an area as big as Windermere, where sailing, fishing and the study of wildlife are enjoyed, not only by the local population, but by many people from other counties. Belvoir Castle, home of the Dukes of Rutland, and Bradgate Park to the west of Leicester, where Lady Jane Grey once lived, are rich in history. Perhaps the most famous historical attraction is Bosworth Field where Richard III lost his crown at the Battle of Bosworth in 1485.

The members of the Women's Institutes have enjoyed piecing together a picture of their villages of contrasting size and character. They hope that all who read this book will find pleasure in the variety of life, both past and present, in Leicestershire and Rutland.

Anthea Kenyon
Federation Chairman

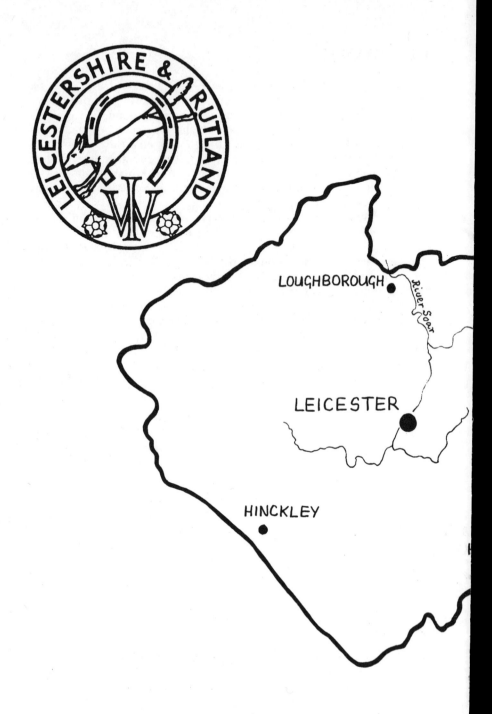

LOUGHBOROUGH

River Soar

LEICESTER

HINCKLEY

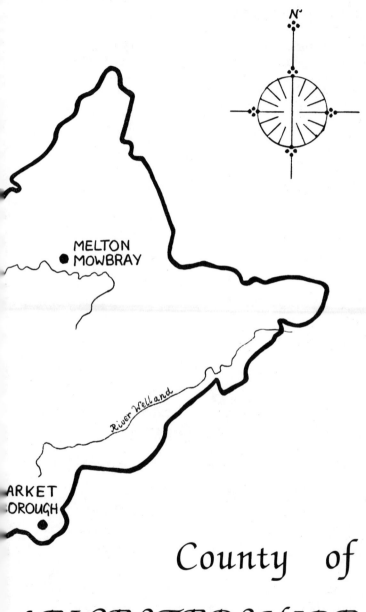

N'

MELTON
MOWBRAY

River Welland

ARKET
OROUGH

County of

LEICESTERSHIRE

Acknowledgements

The Leicestershire and Rutland Federation of Women's Institutes would like to thank all those members and others who have worked so hard to produce the text and drawings in this book. A special thank you to Stella Elliott who co-ordinated the project, assisted by Diana Trotter.

Packhorse Bridge, Anstey

Ab Kettleby 🥨

Ab Kettleby is a pleasant village situated on the A606 road, three miles from Melton Mowbray and 15 miles south-east of Nottingham. In the 1930s, at the burial of a vicar, a quantity of Roman mosaic tiles were discovered.

On entering Ab Kettleby observe the old village inn, probably 17th century, with the unusual name of The Sugar Loaf. Further down the village street, an ancient house stands on the corner (the home of the Freckingham family for over 400 years). It is built of local ironstone with some of the original mullioned windows. Other houses are also built of local ironstone and the manor house is built in an unusual cruciform fashion, with a large central brick chimney.

The parish church of St James, mostly 13th century, has many outstanding features. There are some medieval poppy head benches and a striking monument dated 1628 to Everard Digby, a connection of the Digby of Gunpowder Plot fame.

The present Methodist chapel was built 140 years ago and the origins of Methodism here date back around 180 years. A service is held in the chapel every Sunday. The old village spring well with its stone cap is well kept. It formerly supplied the local water needs.

1988 was the 125th anniversary of the opening of the present Ab Kettleby school, although directories record that there was a schoolmaster in the village as early as 1842. Forty children now attend the school, up to the age of eleven years. In 1882 it is recorded that 118 children were attending the school, at the height of local quarrying. Quarrying is recorded as early as 1577 and continued in the parish until 1975. Part of the quarries is now a nature reserve.

In the 18th century Ab Kettleby had a framework knitter. There were very few framework knitter's cottages in this area. In 1800 the co-operatives began and machines were let out on rental and in the returns made between 1800 and 1850 the framework knitter is not recorded.

A windmill is first mentioned in the village in 1326. It is still mentioned in the records in 1880, but not in 1890.

In the past the village was self-supporting with its own carpenter, wheelwright, blacksmith, cobbler, tailor, etc. It had its own bakery and bread was baked there until the 1950s – it is now a private house. The village also had a butcher's shop and slaughterhouse and at least two other shops. Most farmhouses had a cheese room and Stilton was made and sold at the Cheese Fayre. Butter was made, poultry dressed and sold in this area and at Melton and Nottingham markets. Agriculture also played an important part in employment. There were eleven 'milking' farms up to the middle of the 20th century. There are now five farms in the village.

Anstey 🐚

Anstey lies about four miles to the north-west of Leicester, and has a population of over 6,000. The Saxons, who settled here between the 5th and 8th centuries, knew it as Hanstige, meaning 'the high path'. In 1086 the Domesday Book recorded it as Anstige, and legend claims that the last wolf to be killed in England was shot in a forest near Anstige in Wolfdale. In the early 20th century the spelling was changed from Ansty to Anstey to distinguish it from Ansty near Coventry.

Rothley brook runs through the village, crossed by two notable bridges; the packhorse bridge, which is of medieval origin, and King William's bridge, constructed to facilitate William III's journey along Sheepwash Lane, when he came to visit the Grey family of Bradgate Park in 1696.

Many of Anstey's finest old buildings have now sadly been demolished. The oldest surviving building is Green Farm, dating from the early 15th century. Most of St Mary's parish church was built in 1846, of Charnwood granite and Swithland slate. However, traces of Norman work can be found in the tower and font, the gargoyles are Early English and the stump of a Saxon preaching cross can still be seen in the churchyard. The tenor bell is believed to be the only one in the country to bear the inscription, 'Recast in the year of the accession of King Edward VIII'.

A cobbled pavement of Charnwood granite survives in Park Road, where the old village school has been preserved in its outward form, but converted into flats inside. Many of the trees on the green are diseased or have died, so a new avenue of 18 Canadian red oaks has recently been planted.

The most notable family of Anstey from the 13th century until 1892, when they moved to Woodhouse Eaves, was the Martin family, two of whom were Lord Lieutenants of Leicestershire. The local high school is named after them.

A half-witted Anstey lad, Ned Ludlam or Ned Ludd, gave his name to the Luddites, who in the 1800s followed his earlier example by smashing machinery in protest against the Industrial Revolution.

Anstey has long enjoyed a reputation for charitable work. Each year

Toc H raise money by carol singing at Christmas, to provide an outing for the village's old folk in June. A charitable trust for the benefit of local people was set up by Mary Heard who died in 1803. The value of this has dwindled to such an extent that it now provides the old folk with just two eggs per head at Easter.

For centuries Anstey was primarily an agricultural community. The first industry to arrive was stocking frame knitting. Later it was noted for boot and shoe manufacturing. There are still factories interspersed with the houses, notably box and envelope manufacturers, and a publisher of large print books. These days, however, a majority of people commute to work.

Appleby Magna & Appleby Parva

The villages of Appleby Magna and Appleby Parva lie between the old Roman road of Salt Street and one of the newest motorways, the M42.

William de Appleby settled in Appleby Magna in 1166 and had a stone house built, surrounded by a moat. The gate house, now known as the Moat House, still stands, occupied and lovingly preserved, in the centre of the village.

The village church was built in the 14th century, but was considerably restored by the Victorians. It houses many interesting artefacts, which include the alabaster effigies of Sir Edmund de Appleby and his wife. Fragments of beautiful 14th century glass are to be seen in the windows, and there are Victorian box pews and examples of Victorian graffiti taken from the roof when it was re-leaded.

In the 17th century, the benefactors of the village were the Moore family from Appleby Parva, who resided at Appleby Hall, now sadly demolished. Sir John Moore had made money from the East India spice trade. One time Lord Mayor of London during the reign of Charles II, he had a free grammar school built in the style of Christopher Wren. This was a boarding school for the sons of 'gentlemen' from the surrounding villages. A life size statue of him in his ceremonial robes still stands in an alcove in the school hall. After many years it reopened in the 1950s as a Church of England primary school which it still is today.

After the penny post came in in 1840, a letter box was fixed into a wall of the public house called the Anchor, no longer in existence, in Appleby Parva. A stream ran at the side of the building, past the Octagonal House

11

(still lived in) and over Hall Park to Appleby Hall. Squire Moore, a descendant of Sir John, decided that he would enjoy walking to post his own letters, but did not want to paddle through the stream. He used bricks from derelict cottages to build a culvert for the stream to pass through and had a pathway made over it so that he could walk to post his letters and keep his feet dry.

The Moore family also had a row of almshouses built of hand-made local brick in 1839, opposite the church. Elderly people still live in these now modernised and attractive buildings.

Buildings of interest include several 17th century houses. One of these, The Black Horse, is well worth a visit.

Until the end of the Second World War, the village's only water supply was from hand-pumped wells, many households often sharing the same pump. Rights of way through various gardens still exist because of this. Piped water was installed in most houses by 1953 and the sound of a chain being pulled was sweet music.

Maypole dancing takes place on the car park of the Crown public house, the children of the local school entertaining the public. There is a post office and general store, a village shop, two butcher's shops and three public houses.

Arnesby

Originally a Saxon settlement dating from the late 9th century, Arnesby appears in the Domesday Book as 'Erendesbi'. The village lies just off what was the Leicester–Welford turnpike road, now the A50. A pleasant and compact village, it has two open areas of village green, one of which is shaded by an oak tree planted for the Coronation of George V. Houses are a mixture of styles and ages, including several timber framed cottages, one of which is still thatched. The old manor house in the Church Field, still there in 1860, has now disappeared, leaving only the moat and fishpond to show where it once stood.

The oldest building in the village is St Peter's church. Basically a Norman structure, with additions made in the 13th, 14th and 15th centuries, the whole was extensively restored during the Victorian period.

Inside the building is a tablet commemorating the founding of the Loseby Charity. Established in 1668 this bequest was laid out in land used as allotments. The rent was distributed annually among the needy of the parish. Today this goes to pensioners. Lessening demand for allotments has resulted in most of the land being let to local farmers.

The Manor House at Arnesby

Nonconformists are catered for by the Particular Baptist church. Founded in 1667 the congregation first met in a small building which now provides living accommodation for the minister and his family; while the manse has become a Christian Conference Centre. The present church was built around 1799, with later additions of a vestry and Sunday schools in the mid-19th century.

The Church of England National school was built by subscripton in 1859. Records show a total of 99 pupils when the school began. The old school bell, having been silenced during the Second World War along with the church bells, was restored in 1978 and once again performs its original task. Also important to village life is the village hall, built in the early 1930s as a Men's Institute.

A prominent feature of the village is the windmill, which was refurbished during the 1970s and once more provides a striking landmark for miles around.

Population figures show a wide variation between the 25 of the 11th century and the other extreme of 573 at the 1861 census. Currently the number is around 250. Employment has changed radically since 100 years ago. Then men were either framework knitters or farm labourers and unmarried women were likely to be 'in service'. Today with farms mechanised and other local work having largely disappeared, the majority commute daily to surrounding areas, being engaged in a wide range of jobs.

Sadly, Arnesby no longer has a shop. Before the Second World War the village boasted its own baker, butcher, shoe repairer, a post office cum general store and three other shops. The Old Cock is the sole survivor of three public houses which once existed. A residential home for the elderly now exists too.

All is not loss, however. Early in 1953 mains water replaced village wells and in 1974 sewers were constructed, to the great benefit of all. Improved street lighting, better roads and housing make life both safer and more pleasant.

Asfordby ✤

One hardly hears the name 'Assaby' nowadays but the locals always used it until recent years and it closely resembles the ancient spelling, Assobie.

The church of All Saints was built of local ironstone in the 13th century, the tower added in the 14th and the tall spire in the 15th. The 'Old Hall' is the oldest house in the village, and is said to be haunted by a splendidly uniformed soldier.

The ancient village cross stands by the main street, at the entrance to Church Lane. In the late 1930s a lorry delivering flour to the bakery near the church backed into it, shattering the shaft. It has since been repaired, but the bakery is no more. The only public transport in the early 1900s was a horsedrawn brake owned by the baker. This was used for weddings and even on one occasion was hired for a honeymoon trip around Belvoir Castle!

There are three old inns in the village, The Blue Bell, The Three Horseshoes and The Crown, all still in use. Opposite The Crown is the Church of England school, no longer used as a school, but for many meetings and activities. Captains Close is the new primary school, built August 1971.

Around 1880 Holwell Works became an iron foundry. Houses were built for the employees, also a school. 1962 saw the end of the blast furnaces and the tall chimneys, a landmark for years, were demolished. Pipes are still produced but the workforce is much smaller.

In 1940, during the Second World War, a land mine fell in the valley, causing no damage other than a huge crater in a field. But one early morning in 1941 a German plane dropped a string of bombs along the concrete road, four men on the way to work were killed and the blast damaged the valley houses and killed a small girl, who was in bed.

In the late 1800s there was a mill, but all that is left now is the mill race and a grinding stone lying on the roadside.

A medieval bridge spans the river on Station Lane and the skill of those old builders is proved by the fact that it carries the continuous heavy loads of today's traffic.

Housing estates now encircle the village on all sides and a play area, council allotments and a cemetery are on the outskirts. A £400 million coal superpit is also being built on the outskirts of the village.

Ashby Magna 🌿

Ashby Magna (formerly called Asserby) is described in *White's Directory of Leicestershire and Rutland* (1863) as 'a pleasant village, (it) has in its parish 315 inhabitants and 1,804 acres of land.' The population is about the same today.

The village is not now the self-contained agricultural one it was in 1863. Then there was a church, a school, an inn, a post office, a hosiery maker, a tailor, a grocer, a carpenter, a shoemaker, a bakehouse (where people would take their Sunday dinners to be cooked), a blacksmith and a butcher as well as farmers and their farm workers; of these only the church, the inn and the farmers remain.

Ashby Magna used to be almost self-sufficient – most people grew their own vegetables, fattened their own pig, kept hens and bought their food from the village shops or from the visiting tradesmen. Milk was obtained from the farms, drinking water from wells and springs and 'soft' water (for washing) was collected in water butts. White's Directory also refers to 'a copious spring at the western end of the village, said to be efficacious as a cure for sore eyes.' There are many springs in the village, the waters of which flow northward towards the North Sea, whereas two miles further south, all the streams flow southwards to the Bristol Channel.

Piped water came to the village in 1960, electricity came in the 1920s and a gas supply is just now being brought in.

The parish church of St Mary is described by White as 'a neat structure of decorated architecture with a tower and three bells which in 1860 underwent a thorough restoration at a cost of £400.' The church clock was added in 1937 at the time of King George VI's coronation. Near the church is the moated site of an ancient hall.

Ashby Magna had a railway station on the LNER (Sheffield to London) line. Mrs Cott (the vicar's wife at Ashby Magna, who was also lady of the manor, having been given the parish as a wedding present by her uncle) gave a piece of land for the station. Bricks were made from clay dug from the pits near Brick Yard Lane (now called Holt Lane), near to the village. The line was closed in the 1960s and now the M1 motorway runs alongside it.

At Hubbards Farm, young people are being trained under the Government's Youth Training Scheme, and thus Ashby Magna is making its contribution to the future.

Ashwell ✤

In Saxon times the village was called Exwell. There is a well in a tiny roadside glade as you enter the village, with a rhyming inscription on its stonework canopy below the cross:

'All ye who hither come to drink.
Rest not your thoughts below.
Look at the sacred sign and think
Whence living waters flow.'

The church of St Mary is mainly 14th century. In the north chantry is a life size alabaster effigy of a priest in Church vestments. The figure was once gilded and in the folds of the robes some gilding can still be seen. Wooden effigies are quite rare, but there is one in the south chantry. It is believed to be of Sir Thomas Touchet.

Although no inn exists now, there used to be one called the Tambourine (now Langham Place). It was closed because it became a hideout for poachers. Tambourine bridge still remains.

A Methodist chapel was built in 1913 from money collected by the villagers at a gathering held in Lincolnshire because the Bromleys would not allow nonconformists on the estate. The manor had been handed down through marriage from Viscount Downe, who once owned the village. He also built the school which was closed in the late 1960s. The bell still remaining on the property was last rung for Queen Elizabeth's Jubilee in 1977.

The village had a resident blacksmith, his forge now a garage at a house called the Croft. In the 19th century there was a bakehouse in Water Lane. It had a stick-oven, one which had a fire built in the oven itself and raked out when hot, the dough then being put in for baking. Although the oven has been bricked up it is still visible today. In the same lane is the oldest house in the village, known as home farm.

Ashwell Feast (Sunday after 19th September) was once held on the village green, but by 1870 it was no longer celebrated. Ploughboy Monday also ceased in 1918.

During the Second World War, as the nearest sirens were in Oakham, residents were notified of air raids by Mrs Nellie Tomblin cycling around the village blowing a whistle or ringing a bell. She tells of villagers counting the aeroplanes out as they flew over from Cottesmore airfield on their missions and then counting them back on their return, joyful if the same number came back. The airfield is still being used today.

The village hall doubles as a social club. There is a thriving garage and a village shop cum post office.

A few new houses built makes the population just over 200. Members of the Cottesmore Hunt reside in the village and the hounds are kept just outside at the Cottesmore Kennels. Also a distance from the village is Ashwell Prison. Although there are some who commute to work there is still a healthy nucleus remaining who continue rural activities.

Aylestone 🦋

Aylestone is mentioned in the Domesday Book of 1086, but long before that there was a settlement here. Lying in a hollow beside the river Soar some two miles south-west of Leicester, the site is of undoubted antiquity.

The parish church of St Andrew has stood for well over 700 years. The best known story connected with the church is the legend of the elopement and secret marriage in 1565 of Dorothy Vernon, second daughter of Sir George Vernon of Haddon Hall in Derbyshire, and John Manners, the second son of the Earl of Rutland. There are records of the grandchildren of Dorothy and John being christened in Aylestone church.

Aylestone Hall was in the possession of the Dukes of Rutland until 1869 when it was sold to the Stretton family. During the Second World War it was requisitioned by the Army, and was left in a very bad state at the end of the war. It was taken over by Leicester Corporation in 1950, who have turned the grounds into a beautiful little park, with tennis courts and bowling greens.

The old National school still stands in the village, a little red brick building surrounded by iron railings, now a dance school. The Granby Road Infants, with its girls and boys entrances, celebrated its centenary in 1989.

There have been some interesting characters living in Aylestone; one of these was Mrs Newman, who kept an old fashioned sweet shop. As Miss Norman she was Captain of the Olympic swimming team around 1905. She was presented with a large silver rose bowl by Vesta Tilly. She lived to a great age, and at 90 was still swimming.

17

Aylestone village is a very pleasant place to live in today; only 20 minutes bus ride to the city centre. It is well served with shops and has three pubs, The Black Horse, The Union and The Rutland.

The Great Central Way, the old railway line, has been made into a walkway; one can also walk through the Aylestone Meadows (a botanist's delight) or along the towpath right into the city centre.

Barkby 🌿

Barkby is a small village standing five miles north-east from the centre of Leicester, with approximately 330 residents. The village was enclosed in 1779 and little has changed since then, with only eight new properties being built since the 1960s. The brook still winds its way through the village providing pleasure to young and old alike, not to mention the resident ducks.

The farms of this agricultural village are mainly arable, with five dairy herds ranging from 80 to 150 cows. Only a small number of the residents now work on the land, as compared to the majority prior to the 1950s, most people now commuting to work in Leicester.

The decline of the rural agricultural connection is reflected in the change of use of the village blacksmith and the wheelwright's shop. In the 1800s farm carts were made on the premises and horses waiting to be shod were a common sight, often tethered outside in the main street. Wrought iron work was also carried out and the church gates, still in use today, were made there. The wheelwright's shop has long since closed, but the blacksmith's shop is still in use as an engineering works, as is the former village bakery which now manufactures components for the shoe trade.

In the centre of the village, surrounded by parkland stands Barkby Hall, owned and lived in by the Pochin family, who for many centuries have been benefactors in the village. In 1707 a schoolmaster to teach ten of the infant poor was appointed and in 1826 George Pochin built a school.

Barkby has one village shop and post office and a telephone box, which are well supported by local residents. Barkby is also fortunate in having its own cricket field, an attractive site in the centre of the village.

Refreshment for villagers is provided by two public houses, strategically placed one at each end of the village. The older is the Malt Shovel Inn, where the beer was actually brewed on the premises, the other being the Brookside.

The village church of St Mary, mentioned in 1200 and situated in the centre of the village, has an almost square nave with wide side aisles, giving the impression of great space. The present patrons are the Pochin's of Barkby Hall, who over the years have helped with its upkeep.

Barkby Thorpe is a hamlet situated a third of a mile from Barkby. It consists of twelve homes, all but one belonging to the Pochin estate.

There is a well known pond, Abbots Pond, built by the abbots of Leicester to supply fish for their table. This was also the site of the fruit market, for selling fruit grown in the orchards. The field is known as Cherry Orchard. There are 15 known wells, one of which supplied water for Barkby Hall.

Beeby is situated about two miles from Barkby. It sits in a basin formed by several hills. It consists of several council owned houses, three farms, a few private houses and a manor house. The centre is taken up by All Saints church, containing all three styles of Gothic architecture. Beeby has one well, which can still be seen alongside the main street.

Barrow-upon-Soar 🦕

The twin delights of a riverside setting and the nearby Charnwood Forest bring holiday-makers to Barrow-upon-Soar each year. The village emblem, the plesiosaurus fossil found here in 1851, recalls roots even deeper in history than the name 'Barhoo', used for the Norman manor with its three working mills mentioned in the Domesday Book.

Working mills continued from the Middle Ages to the days of the stone-crushing water-driven wheels which still turned at the end of Mill Lane into the present century. One villager remembers watching, as a girl, the heavy-laden barges bringing the gypsum rock to be processed for building. Gypsum and lime beneath the fields gave mining work to generations of local men, while stocking-knitters' frames were used in scores of village cottages. Barrow's work today is not so village-centred: many living in the newer estates circling the old streets travel daily to Loughborough, Leicester, Nottingham or Derby.

The lively community still surprises newcomers with its variety of activities, in a tradition of self-reliance witnessed by photos of Victorian outings, celebrations and entertainments. There are three social clubs, including one for the over-60s. Once there were ten pubs – now there are only seven!

The glorious medieval parish church of the Holy Trinity, enriched with fine carving by the renowned local craftsman Jack Hinds, hosts concerts and recitals. It shares with the Methodist, Baptist and Roman Catholic congregations the continuing Christian worship and service which originally produced the village primary schools and the high school.

Eminent Barrow men of the past gave their names to streets and buildings. Beveridge Street, a conservation area, has unspoilt examples of fine houses, from the 600 year old Bishop Beveridge's House, where the Bishop of St Asaph was born in 1636, to the present century. Local legend tells of an underground passage from the Bishop's House to the parish church at the top of the street. One scholar and benefactor, Humphrey Babington, founded the Old Men's Hospital, now trust-run flats, from which the robed bedesmen walked across to enter the church by their own special door from 1694 until the 1930s.

The river Soar and the canal give pleasant meadows, a fine bridge, good fishing and tow path walks. The river sometimes floods, cutting the Barrow to Quorn road, and in 1912 produced the highest floodwater for a century.

Well-remembered Barrow residents include Theophilus Cave, whose devotion to his church inspired Humphrey Babington's bequest of 'Cave Bibles' for children of the parish – a bequest still honoured annually. A popular Barrow saying was, 'Lucky, like Mr Monk'. Mr Monk, a cobbler, made himself a pair of leather wings, and jumped off his apple tree in the conviction that he could fly. He came to no worse harm than landing in the mud.

Barrowden ✤

The 'barrows' (burial mounds) of the village name may be those to be seen to the north-east of the village.

St Peter's church is situated at the south-west end of the village, not far from the picturesque main green and duck pond. The ancient custom of 'rush-bearing' is still observed at the Patronal Festival each year, when the church floor is strewn with rushes gathered from the banks of the nearby river Welland.

In 1829, a Thomas Cook met Marianne Mason, a farmer's daughter living at West Farm, Barrowden. He was an itinerant Baptist missionary, but due to a lack of funds, he became a wood turner and cabinet-maker. They married in 1833 and moved to Market Harborough. On 5th July 1841, they hired a special train to take some Leicester Temperance supporters to a rally at Loughborough. This was the foundation of the Thomas Cook travel agency.

A water mill is mentioned in 1259, and was probably the site on which the 1637 mill was constructed by Mr Bullingham, on the river Welland. This mill has now been demolished, but a survey made in 1955 of the various dates etched on the inside of the remaining wall, revealed: 1677, 1688, BF 1705, and 1787. 'BF' is thought to refer to 'The Big Flood', as lines were cut in against that date. Floods must have been higher than any in living memory, and it is suggested that this was before the fens were drained. These etched stones and a mill stone now decorate a garden in the Old Tannery Yard.

Behind the mill was the tannery, where hides from local cows were processed to make rugs, parchment for drums and also glue. The tannery closed in 1885, but an outbuilding was turned into a large shop by Mr Kirby, who toured villages selling his various goods. When Mr Kirby died in 1934, the contents of the shop were sold by auction.

The old shop, and Mr Kirby's house were bought by Mr Frank Ellis, who converted and drove what is believed to have been the first motorised travelling fish and chip van in the country. During the Second World War, the old tannery was used as a factory, making ammunition cases, and in recent years, as a plastics factory. Sadly in 1986, it was demolished to make way for new houses.

In 1900 there were three bakehouses, five shops, three butchers, four shoemakers, three tailors, two smiths, and five public houses. Tippings Lane took its name from the blacksmith, who worked on the green in the 19th century. Besides his usual work, he made muzzle-loading guns. Kings Lane is named after a tailor who lived there.

Many present villagers can recall taking the Sunday joints to be roasted, at 2d a time, in the huge oven of the last remaining bakehouse, which has now been converted into a home. The village school closed in the 1960s, and has also suffered the same fate.

Fortunately, one shop remains, combining the post office counter with the traditional village shop goods and service. The shop provides some free groceries each month for many elderly residents, under two village charities. One was set up by Mr John Brown in 1833, who left property in Hammersmith, the other by the rector's daughter, Mary Cary, who in 1876 left invested money, which also provides some free coal each winter to qualifying pensioners.

Barwell 🌿

Barwell is said to date back to before Roman times. In the past, when building work was in progress, burnt flay stones, pot boilers, horns and bones were found. Bronze Age fragments and a cinerary urn belonging to the later Bronze Age have also been unearthed. Mentioned in the Domesday Book as Berryall, later the spelling changed to Bearwell.

Barwell grew rapidly with industry around the turn of the 19th century when the shoe trade came to town. A local man, George Ward, is well remembered in the community for his shoe factory. He also purchased a property on Shilton Road called The Cedars, as a community centre for the people of Barwell.

St Mary's church is the oldest building, Anglo-Saxon in origin. A story told by locals has Richard III's soldiers sharpening their swords and lances on the cornerstones of the church. The marks can be seen to this day. Outside the church stands the 'wandering' war memorial. This landmark used to be in what is known as Top Town (although the reason for this name is not clear, it is the more central part of present day Barwell).

The most interesting places other than this are now all public houses. The Queens, the oldest building on High Street, has only in the past century become a pub. The Cross Keys has close associations with the church, the key to the church can be seen behind the bar waiting to let travellers in. Running down the side of the house is what is left of a cobbled path which led across the common to the church and by which access can still be gained. The Three Crowns, again in High Street, was a coaching inn for travellers. One coachhouse and stable can be seen at the rear of this hostelry.

The Blacksmith's Arms in Top Town was one of the two blacksmith's shops, the other having been sadly lost to the developers.

Belton in Rutland 🌿

Belton in Rutland lies on a hillside 500 ft above sea level and has an area of 1,024 acres. The village consists of 122 houses, many built since 1950.

King Charles I is believed to have rested in Belton after the Battle of Naseby in 1645 and the stone base of the war memorial is still known as the King's Stone. In 1920 the then Prince of Wales often visited the village.

In living memory Belton was a self-sufficient community with two bakehouses, three dairies (one delivering milk daily in jugs), a butcher's shop and slaughterhouse, a draper's shop, a post office and two grocery shops, three village pubs, a blacksmith's, several dressmakers—tailors, an undertaker, chimney sweep, greengrocery shop, a laundry, and a coal merchant. There were tennis courts, cricket and football fields and a lot of keen sportsmen and women.

The Church of England gave the land and the village school was built by public subscription in 1870. Famous teachers were Mr Crabbe, who taught for 31 years and his wife, who taught for 43 years. The school closed in 1971 and now the building is used as a playschool.

Today the village still possesses a post office/general stores and two public houses. A van selling fresh fish calls every Friday and there is still daily delivery of fresh milk, but it now comes from Melton Mowbray. A mobile library van calls every fortnight and a bus service has been re-routed to come through the village, after a local petition.

There were many festivals celebrated in the village in the past. Belton Club feast was held on Whit Monday and was organised by the Ancient Order of Foresters with a parade through the village, a travelling fair and sideshows and ending with a dance at night in the Black Horse.

On Ploughboy Monday youngsters would black their faces and go round the village collecting money. May Day celebrations were held in the school and playground with maypole dancing, parades round the village and the crowning of the May Queen in the village hall with a tea for all to end the day. The Feast of St James the Apostle was held on or around 25th July, when a fair and circus was held every year at the top of Goughs Lane from 1330 until the First World War.

St Peter's church dates back to the 13th century with parts of it even earlier. The pews were made by the village carpenter and can seat 200 people.

Billesdon

Billesdon Coplow is on the old Bronze Age route from Stamford through Tilton into the Soar valley. Anglo-Saxons were probably the first settlers here, possibly initially on the Coplow then moving down to the sheltered valley below where Billesdon now stands. A fine brooch of the mid-6th century was found on the site of a burial mound near the village.

Billesdon's greatest period of growth was during the second half of the

16th century when it became a small market centre. Its population grew from 38 families in 1563 to 154 in 1603. In 1618 Billesdon had two fairs and a weekly Friday market. The market cross in the present Market Place is partly medieval and now an ancient monument.

The oldest surviving houses in the village are of cruck construction, of local ironstone, and date from the 17th century. By the end of the 18th century Billesdon had its own brickworks and several of the brick houses round the Market Place date from this time.

During the early 19th century most of Billesdon's inhabitants were in occupations which were mainly rural, such as farm labourers, corn millers, farmers etc, or those providing a service for the village, such as shopkeepers, bakers, publicans, schoolmasters, carriers or postmasters. Framework knitting was at its height between 1850 and 1890, with the wives being employed in allied occupations such as stocking seaming or glove stitching.

The advent of the Billesdon Hunt in 1838 saw the increase of grooms, blacksmiths and vets for the southern part of the Quorn, which later became the Fernie Hunt.

Many of the present inhabitants of Billesdon travel daily to Leicester to work, although 'Syston Tooling and Design' in the village provides a little employment within the community.

Billesdon was the home of the famous horse-breaker Thomas Tomblin – popularly called Captain Tomblin. He was described in White's Directory 1846 as 'the cleverest rough-rider in the world' who could 'reduce to

The Old School House, Billesdon

tractability the most spirited and obstinate animals, where other breakers have failed'.

In 1829 Captain Becher, known as 'the Father of Gentlemen Riders', had his original mount in the first cross-country contest in England in which a representative field took part. This was from Noseley Wood to Billesdon Coplow. This was won by Mr Field Nicholson on Sir Harry Goodricke's *Magic*. Captain Becher was unplaced, but his name will always be remembered in connection with Aintree's Grand National race and the famous brook that is called after him.

Billesdon church was given to Leicester Abbey early in the 12th century and this made the Abbey owners of land and property in Billesdon. The earliest surviving part of the church around the base of the tower dates from before 1250.

Billesdon General Baptist chapel was built in 1812. 1846 saw the opening of the Salem chapel in West Lane for Particular Baptists and in 1854 the Wesleyans built a chapel in Church Street. Of these only the Baptist chapel remains.

In 1650 William Sharpe of Rolleston endowed a free school for the parish – although it is thought that the old school building is older. In 1895 the building was being run by a group of local shareholders as a village institute with library–reading room and 'Appliances for Recreation'!

Birstall 🐾

Birstall village is about three miles from Leicester, a fact which has influenced its development. The village is situated on rising ground on the banks of the river Soar.

The road from Leicester to Loughborough passed by the village and very little seems to have disturbed life in this backwater until the Leicester Navigation canalised the river Soar. The villagers' opinion of the canal people is perhaps reflected in the tale of the Shag-dog, a large black mastiff reputed to live in Shag-dog pit near the river. A young girl from Birstall had to walk to Belgrave to ask the doctor to visit a sick friend. It was dark when she returned and hearing footsteps behind her, she turned to see a rough-looking bargee following. Suddenly a dog barked and the Shag-dog appeared. He walked at her side and the man's footsteps stopped. When the girl arrived home, the dog disappeared. The next day the bargee could not be found.

Birstall's population did not change dramatically until the 20th century. In 1830, 199 people lived here: in 1851 the number was 491. In

1899 the Great Central Railway opened and Birstall gained a railway station, although it was about a mile from the village. Houses were built near to the station and 'New Birstall' developed away from the old village centre. By 1931 over 3,000 people lived here. This number had increased to 12,000 by 1970 when the last estate was completed.

Few old buildings remain, but the church, originally built in the 13th century, still stands in an extended and renovated form. Evidence of an Anglo-Saxon church on this site is provided by remnants of a latticework window and the Birstall 'Beast', a stone carving of an unidentified animal which was brought to light about 50 years ago. The church was restored in 1869 and enlarged in 1961.

Two 15th century houses still exist, but of the large houses of the village, only two remain. Goscote Hall was last used as an hotel, and The Holt is now a children's home. The large houses in Birstall were usually occupied by businessmen from Leicester. Birstall was considered a desirable place to live away from the busy town. John Mansfield, a notable banker, lived at Birstall House; Mr Walker of The Holt was a boot and hosiery manufacturer. John Coupland, at one time Master of the Quorn Hunt, resided at Goscote Hall.

As the village grew, local facilities were increased. The old village school, built of Mountsorrel granite in 1860 was replaced by new buildings in the 1930s. It is now the church hall. Two additional junior schools and two secondary schools were built more recently.

Leicestershire County Council are currently developing disused gravel pits near the river into a country park, and Birstall may soon become a recreational haven for walking, birdwatching and fishing.

Bitteswell 🦙

Betmeswelle, as it appears in the Domesday Book of 1086, means 'the stream or spring at the head of the valley'. It is a village with central greens crossed by its main thoroughfares, forming a crossroads in the centre. The greens, the clearings made by the first Saxon settlers and surrounded by its cottages and houses, have been jealously guarded over the years.

From a strictly rural settlement it has progressed over the centuries to a lively community of mixed age groups with almost all those of working age being occupied outside the village. There are still several farming families, who get their living from the land; cattle, sheep and poultry being the main products. A good proportion is arable farming which has existed since the Second World War. Prior to that it was mostly pasture and there were a number of smallholders who kept cows and sold their dairy produce. Now there is not one single milking cow within the parish.

But this is still a complete village – it has its own church, standing on the edge of the greens; and it has a school, which has celebrated its centenary. There is a combined shop and post office, a village hall, a Women's Institute, a Mothers' Union and a Friendship Club for the elderly. A daily bus service operates through the neighbouring villages and to Lutterworth and beyond and a mobile library visits every fortnight. There are two hostelries and a cricket club of long standing with its own pitch on the outskirts.

The village contains two thatched houses and a number of Georgian dwellings, all well preserved. Modern houses mix amicably with the old. Population figures have not altered much since records began in 1801. Then 398 souls were recorded as against about 380 today. In 1841 there was a big increase caused by the building of Bitteswell Hall, north of the village. This brought employment and new families as it had its own farms, gas installation etc, but in the 1920s it was demolished, the land and buildings split up and the population went down to an all-time low at 293.

An item in a newspaper of 1791 tells the following story: A man from Bitteswell sold his wife for the sum of half a crown. According to the report, 'she was publickly delivered in a Halter at 12 o'clock the said day in the market at Lutterworth amidst a concourse of many hundreds of people'. What the vicar of the time thought of it is not recorded. This was the Rev James Powell, a great benefactor to the parish, who served here for 55 years. It was his wife, formerly Mary Twining, who was responsible for introducing the famous tea family to the parish. Members of the family still lived here until 1906.

The Second World War brought a great upheaval. Land on the west side of the village was taken over and an airfield built to train aircrews. At the end of the war it became a prisoner of war camp for Italians and then Germans and finally a temporary haven for the displaced persons from Eastern Europe. It was eventually taken over by British Aerospace and some of the most modern jet planes were regular visitors. But all that is in the past. A big new development, which spreads over many hundreds of acres and encroaches into other parishes, is taking place. This area has been named Magna Park, a huge distribution complex which may eventually have its own housing and leisure centre.

Blaby 🌿

Blaby is a typical village with its roots firmly in the past. The name derives from a Norse word 'blae', meaning blue, dark and cheerless. It lies five miles south of Leicester and has a population of about 7,000. Although it has grown continuously since 1945 there is still a little open countryside on the outskirts of the village.

The older part still gives some indication of the past. The first Baptist meeting house was built in 1807, and until 1812 worshippers walked down to the river Sence for baptism, where a bend in the river was known as 'Little Jordan'. A new chapel was dedicated in 1876 and this has been completely refurbished.

The rector of the parish from 1744–98 was Edward Stokes, who as the result of an accident with a pistol at the age of eight was totally blind. Despite this he was said to be of a 'merry and cheerful disposition'. He enjoyed hunting; a person accompanied him to ring a bell when a 'leap' was to be taken. He established the Stokes Charity to pay for bibles and books for the children and for the repair of the town pump.

The exterior of Ye Olde Bakers Arms, thought to date from 1485, has changed little. It is a timber framed, thatched pub, lovingly preserved, the old ovens now being housed in a small outbuilding.

The census of 1851 shows the beginnings of an industry here: the making of woollen hose. The workers appear to have been extremely independent and, unlike workers in neighbouring villages, they refused to work through a 'bag-man' whose job it was to collect their work, preferring instead to walk into Leicester each week with the results of their labours. Unfortunately the houses where they lived and worked (recognised by their long low windows) have been demolished.

Later, boots and shoes were manufactured and there are still two shoe factories in the village.

In the 1930s Blaby was well known for tomatoes. A large tomato farm supplied produce to many parts of the country. This farm was later sold and a large housing estate was built.

The recent development of an industrial park on the fringe of the village reopened its involvement with food produce as there is now a depot for ripening and storing bananas.

For many years Blaby suffered severe flooding whenever there was heavy rain. Often families were unable to leave their homes, schools were closed (to the delight of the children) and a great deal of misery was caused. During the 1950s a flood prevention scheme was completed, much to everyone's relief. However, it stopped the game played by small boys who, when the water had receded, dared each other to run along the dark, dank culverts.

Blackfordby 🏵

The village of Blackfordby lies about three miles west of Ashby-de-la-Zouch and six miles from Burton-on-Trent. It is an old village and is supposed to have taken its name from the black ford where the village brook crosses the main street after flowing over a coal outcrop. Early maps, such as one dated 1587, show it as 'Blougherby' and this name still survives in the village slang.

The village exists because of the spring and was built around it. The spring water is famous for its clarity and purity. It has never been known to dry up and was the main source of water until the 1930s when mains water arrived. Local people can still be seen calling at it for a drink of 'real' water and it is occasionally bottled for people who are sick.

St Margaret's church dominates the village and the flat land to the south. It is a comparatively modern building, built in 1858 of sandstone which was blackened by the South Derbyshire smoke. It was built near the top of the hill, at a site previously occupied by an earlier 'chapel' which was attached to the Ashby-de-la-Zouch parish church.

Until recently five thatched cottages built in the 16th or early 17th century had survived. Two of the houses were demolished within living memory and one was modernised and fitted with a tiled roof. The two surviving cottages are now protected buildings and one, in the main street, is a much photographed and painted house.

The recreation ground is reputed to be a medieval burial ground and the old people referred to it as the 'old yard'.

For many years the village had a static population of about 500 people. The men were agricultural workers initially but gradually the coal and clay industries of South Derbyshire became the main sources of work both for men and young women.

Blackfordby is still a quiet dormitory village set in rural surroundings but its size has more than doubled. Some new council houses have been built since the Second World War but mainly private development has changed its character. The village school, built in 1889, survives for children up to eight years old. The coal and clay industries have declined and rubber, biscuits, engineering and also the service industries predominate. Some villagers work at the East Midlands airport. The two public houses cater for the village and there is a general stores/post office.

Botcheston
& Newtown Unthank

The hamlet of Botcheston was mentioned in the Domesday Book but nothing is then known about it until 1563 when it is recorded that there were five dwellings. Two cottages, later converted to a coaching inn, were built round a tree and this tree trunk can still be seen in the Greyhound public house.

Between 1751 and 1800 there were framework knitters in the hamlet. Most of the land in Botcheston was farmland and there were few houses until after 1950. There was a school built in the village in 1903 and this was used until the Second World War, when it became a store for the Education Dept. It was given to the village by the Desford Parish Council for use as a village hall in 1970.

In 1965 a plaque was erected in a field in the village by the Clerk to the Duchy of Lancaster to commemorate the 600th anniversary of the founding of the Duchy.

There are still signs in the village of the old brickyard, where the bricks to build the original houses were made out of clay. 'Wayside' was one of the original cottages of the village and used to have a thatched roof. This was built in the 1600s. Hope Cottage is also one of the very early cottages, probably built in the 1800s to house farm workers.

Newtown Unthank in 1920 had 13 dwelling houses, a water mill with accommodation for the miller and a railway station which was one of the early railways constructed by Stephenson. There was also a house for the stationmaster. The latter were known as Desford station and Desford mill, the mill having been built in 1340. The boundary between Desford and Newtown Unthank was the stream known as Rothley brook.

The name Unthank is unusual and it has been suggested that it meant the unthankful, infertile nature of the soil.

The mill has now been converted into a house. Farming is still the main occupation, although there are now a number of professional people living in this very attractive village of twelve houses.

Braunston-in-Rutland 🌿

Braunston-in-Rutland lies on the edge of the old royal hunting forest of Leighfield and its ring shape shows that it started life as a forest clearing. Although there are no longer deer in the forest, the Cottesmore Hunt meet in the village each season.

All Saints church was built between 1150 and the 1400s, the chancel arch being the earliest and the tower the latest building, except for the 19th century vestry. There are vestiges of medieval wall paintings in the south aisle and two brasses to the Cheseldynes, whose farmhouse in the High Street has an armorial dalmation on its datestone.

Several of the larger houses in the village were refurbished in Elizabethan times. Quaintree House with its cedar trees was a medieval hall, enlarged and reclad in stone in the 16th century. Chestnut Farm and Chapter Farm in Wood Lane were probably 'modernised' in the same era, the latter having a garderobe built into an upstairs room which eventually caused the whole gable end to bulge out.

The river Gwash flows through the village and countless generations of children have fished for tiddlers below the sluice or swum in the pools above the village. Near the brook is the village hall, built in the early 1920s as a war memorial to those who fell in the First World War, on land given by Mrs Hanbury of the manor, who lost her son. Mr Hanbury is said to have erected the large clock on the church tower so that his farm-men working down the Brooke Road could see the time. Certainly it can be read from a considerable distance.

Many of the villagers were employed on the land until recently. Even after the Second World War there were three milking herds in the village. The cows wending their leisurely way from field to milking shed blocked the road twice daily. The wives were skilled pork pie and brawn makers and cheeses too if there was a glut of milk. Then there were two general shops, a post office (with public telephone before the days of kiosks), butcher and baker. Now alas, all are gone with the exception of the post office shop.

Until the Second World War, housewives carried their Sunday joint (covered with a white cloth) to the bakery to be roasted while they were in church. Few cottages had electricity or running water, other than a pump into a stone sink and many had no proper oven, cooking being done over an open fire. The blacksmith's forge became a bicycle workshop and is now the garage and two pubs remain of the nine beer shops mentioned at the turn of the century. The manor is a leatherwork factory employing local labour but most of the village workforce commute to Leicester, Peterborough and beyond.

The old school, now a house, stands at the entrance to the churchyard and the curate was paid a small sum out of charity funds to teach twelve poor children free. At one time a hundred pupils were taught in this little building, the younger ones being 'stacked' in a gallery. A new school was built in Knossington Road in 1905 – now a house also – but the old charities remain. These still dispense coal at Christmas time, the trustees meeting on the longest and shortest days of the year. No longer, however, is the church bell rung on St Thomas's Day (21st Dec) for the recipients to queue up in the church porch to receive bread and ale. Nor is charity money used 'for the repair and amendment of decayed bridges and highways'.

Braunstone 🪶

A surprising amount of the character of Braunstone has survived in spite of the fact that a large housing estate has been built on its doorstep.

Fortunately Braunstone is protected by a preservation order, so it remains very much a village, complete with a green. The road through the village is winding and carries a great deal of traffic. Many of the farm workers' cottages are still standing and lived in and some of the inhabitants remember the days when Major Winstanley and his family lived at the Hall, which is now a school.

The school and schoolhouse have been preserved. The school itself has been converted to a house. These buildings are alongside the green. On the other side is a row of farm workers' cottages, restored in 1975–1976 by the City of Leicester to mark European Architectural Year. Along with trees which have been planted on the green, this area makes a very pleasing and attractive approach coming down the lane from Hinckley Road.

The Shakespeare farm has now been converted into a public house but still retains its thatched roof. There was no public house in Braunstone village before this. The field at the rear is a playing field for football, tennis and bowls and the barn is used by the local scout group as their headquarters.

Manor Farm is now a protected building. The house is Elizabethan and the farm buildings have been converted into offices and store sheds from which farming chemicals are sold. The village pump was near to the house but this was removed some years ago.

St Peter's church observes Hay Sunday – it is said that a daughter of the lord of the manor became lost in Aylestone and was found by the clerk of Braunstone church and restored safely to her family. In gratitude, her father gave the hay from one of his fields to be strewn in the church. The verger still receives money in lieu. Amongst the ancient gravestones in the churchyard, one receives much interest:

'Here lyeth ye body of Richard Parsons deceased
ye 30th of March 1683 aged 30.
Is Parsons dead?
Yea, stab'd by wicked Lane
and must lye here till all men rise againe
By Lane's infernal stabb young Parson's dy'd,
Cause in a 'fray he with his friend did side.'

Broughton Astley

Broughton Astley was first mentioned in the Domesday Book in 1086 but was then three separate villages, Broctone, Sutone and Torp, of some 100 persons. Now with a population of over 5,000 and still growing, this one time straggling village will soon be bigger than nearby Lutterworth. The three villages are known today as Broughton Astley, Sutton-in-the-Elms and Primethorpe, now joined together by extensive development and known collectively as Broughton Astley.

The Baptist church was founded in 1650. The small building to the right is the original chapel called the 'Mother of the Baptist Chapels in Leicestershire', where the first meetings took place. Today it is used as the vestry. In the days of religious persecution secrecy was of the utmost and no singing was allowed. As the church in Sutton was hidden by an abundance of elm trees the name as we know it today, Sutton-in-the-Elms, may have derived from this. It was only in 1853 that the baptistry was made into a chapel.

The small graveyard which is still used almost touches the village bypass, which effectively separates this end of the village, and as yet Sutton-in-the-Elms has very little new housing.

Still in Sutton-in-the-Elms lies Quaker Cottage, where some of the earliest Quaker meetings took place as long ago as 1679. Today it isn't wise to dig too deeply into the garden for fear of unearthing old bones, as happened not so long ago. They were replaced and left to rest.

St Mary's church is beautiful and the earliest record is dated 1220,

Baptist chapel of Sutton-in-the-Elms, Broughton Astley

although it must have existed long before that. It is a large stone building and is a mixture of styles and periods.

Thomas Estley High School and Community College opened in September 1976. The name Thomas Estley was chosen because Thomas de Estley was the first patron of St Mary's church in 1220. Other examples of keeping old names are Wilsmer Close and Popple Close, two new road names in Broughton Astley on one of the estates, both named after past railway stationmasters.

Arkwright House was opened in 1981 and is sheltered accommodation for some 35 residents. It was named after Arthur William Arkwright of Broughton Hall, who donated a plate which hangs on the chancel north wall and the carved reredos in St Mary's church.

The railway station used to be in old Broughton, but was sadly closed in the early 1960s. The line in one direction passed through Leire and Ullesthorpe to Rugby and the other way through Countesthorpe and South Wigston to Leicester and then on to Hunstanton. Going on holiday was an adventure not to be missed, with the train journey being the 'icing on the cake', but the age of village steam has long since passed. Station Road and anywhere past the Bull's Head crossroads is today still referred to as 'up station'.

Bruntingthorpe 🐦

Bruntingthorpe, population 422, together with Arnesby and Shearsby, forms part of a gentle, triangular grouping of villages in what must now be one of the few remaining unspoilt areas of South Leicestershire. Its position is approximately eleven miles south of the City of Leicester, on the main A50, which was formerly the old turnpike road of the 1760s and, before that, the chief medieval route linking Leicester and Northampton.

A local distinction is made between Upper and Lower Bruntingthorpe, even though no physical or parish boundary exists. Upper Bruntingthorpe is generally understood to refer to the 600 acre site of the former wartime airfield, and residential development which later grew up alongside it during the 1950s, when the airfield was occupied by the USAF as part of the NATO commitment. During this period, the airfield's runways were greatly extended, and are, in fact, the longest in Europe.

Archaeological evidence suggests that Bruntingthorpe was originally an early Anglo-Saxon settlement, but recent discoveries indicate a much earlier habitation. It was certainly further enlarged by an influx of Viking settlers in the 9th century AD and it is from this period that the village takes its name.

At some point during the late Middle Ages, the original settlement, which is in the fields of Manor Farm, adjacent to St Mary's church, was abandoned in favour of the site of the present village. It is thought that the original site was abandoned after the plague had depopulated it.

In mid-19th century Bruntingthorpe was a prosperous community of 423 people engaged in farming and allied trades. Craftsmen, tradesmen, victuallers, carriers, butchers and bakers, all served the needs of a thriving village. Not least, the stocking frame industry had found its way into most cottages and supplemented many an agricultural wage.

Approaching Lower Bruntingthorpe from Arnesby, one is first of all aware of the gentle ridge and furrow pastures and grazing beasts. Grange Farm is one of the few surviving farms and belongs to the Baker family, probably the oldest farming interest in the parish. They jointly farm about 700 of Bruntingthorpe's 1,200 acres.

Several fine examples of tall, elegant, red brick houses remain; Beresford House and Bruntingthorpe House and the Meet House are but a few. They are set well back and surrounded by walled gardens, with original wrought ironwork. Struggling for recognition alongside such grandeur are the former Baptist chapel (1846) and village school (1871).

Still on Main Street, a beautifully restored early 18th century tithe barn (1717) forms part of a property known as 'White House Farm'. Sadly, no longer a farm, but the barn itself is now used to house 'Stablecare', a business designed to meet all equestrian needs.

The old rectory and restored coach house stand within walking distance of the church. Time has made no significant impact on these beautiful buildings in this quiet corner of the village. St Mary's is a simple church in an idyllic setting; 12th century in origin and totally restored in 1872.

Buckminster & Sewstern

The villages of Buckminster and Sewstern form one parish, both civil and ecclesiastical, with the ancient church of St John the Baptist at Buckminster being the parish church, and the Victorian church at Sewstern being, since 1840, a chapel of ease.

At one time an older church may have existed in Sewstern, but if it did, it has disappeared without a trace, leaving no record of any kind. This is a pity, as Sewstern is a village steeped in history, with the old pre-Roman salt road passing through it. This is known as the Sewstern Lane.

Buckminster, however, is very fortunate in having an unbroken line of vicars since 1222 when Geoffrey was installed, with Baldric as his patron.

Amongst the most renowned parish clergy were the Dixons, who for three generations served the church in the 17th and 18th centuries. (This was apart from the two year incumbency of John Burman 1718–1720). Most famous of these was Samuel Dixon, who was vicar from 1641–95. He it was who built the vicarage, entering in the registers which he kept so accurately and with meticulous neatness. 'This yeare, (namely 1651) I, Samuel Dixon, Vicar of Buckminster, built the Vicaridge-house new from the grounde. To God alone by the glory.'

Samuel was followed by his son, John Dixon (vicar from 1695–1718) and grandson Edward (from 1720–1764).

At the time when the Dixons were serving the parish as clergy, another celebrated family, the Storers were living in Buckminster. Dr Storer appears to have been a most loved and highly respected physician. He is buried on the south side of the choir. He apparently had a very large family as the baptismal registers record at least twelve children.

In the days when primitive conditions prevailed, it must have been a great blessing to the parishioners to have one as skilled as Dr Storer living amongst them and ministering to their health.

Dr Storer was buried in the church on 24th October, 1712, and in 1987, one of his descendants visited the church and his grave.

Burbage

Like many other villages throughout England, Burbage has changed from its original rural aspect to become part of modern suburbia, due to rapid building development.

Burbage Hall is a very beautiful 17th century building, some of its room walls being said to have been hung with tapestries at one time, and it had a concealed priest's hole. The Hall was once the property of the Earls of Gainsborough.

The last of the old Burbage smithies stood near the top of Lychgate Lane, the last horse having been shod there in 1948, when the forge fire went out for the last time.

'The Croft' was once known as The Roebuck Inn. It was a posting house for coaches on the route from London to Derby and Nottingham. In front of The Roebuck Inn was a large pool where the coach drivers would take their horses to drink and cool down after the long journey. The lower end of Church Street still takes its name from that horsepond, namely, 'Horse Pool'!

The church of St Catherine of Alexandria, dating back to the 13th century, lies in the heart of the village, flanked by the parish hall where once the village school was held.

In 1912 it was found that the church steeple was in a dangerous condition. Builders were engaged, scaffolding erected, and work proceeded. During the months of repair it became an accepted challenge for the young men of the village to prove their daring by scaling the ladders and carving their names on the top stones. One day a young lady of 18 decided to attempt the climb. In frilly blouse, long skirts and button boots she ascended safely, inscribed her name and came safely back to terra firma.

In the middle of the 19th century (population approximately 2,000) almost a third of the houses had a hosiery knitting machine to supplement low income. Eventually, hosiery factories were built in the village obviating the need for home knitting. Employees were mainly female but during the 1970s recession and with the incidence of foreign imports, the hosiery industry gradually disappeared in the village.

At the turn of the century Burbage was famed for its beautiful rose gardens and nurseries. These were a favourite venue for Sunday afternoon walks and people came from miles around to admire the flowers and enjoy the delicate perfumes.

In the early years of the century naughty children of the village were threatened by being given to the 'nine o'clock horses'. These beasts toured the village under cover of darkness, pulling carts for the collection of sewage buckets.

An elm was planted in 1887 to commemorate Queen Victoria's Jubilee. This was blown down in 1952 and a search was made for a leaden casket known to be buried there. This contained a parchment deed signed by many villagers, an alamanac dated 1887 and several coins. Alongside this casket are now buried a register of electors of Burbage Ward for 1953, a copy of a newspaper reporting the planting, a souvenir brochure and a set of coins for Coronation Year.

The village has seen great changes in the past decade, as three major housing estates have been developed. In 1985, by special request, Burbage was granted its own Parish Council, which is thought to be the second largest in the whole country.

Burley 🪶

There is some indication that in earlier times much of the village was nearer to Alstoe, now just an outlying farm. Many houses are thought to have been destroyed in Cromwellian times, and the village subsequently rebuilt nearer to the mansion, Burley on the Hill, which at 505 ft above sea level, towers over the countryside. Burley, on the main road between Oakham and Cottesmore, is a straggling village. There is a village green surrounded by a cluster of houses, with more houses bordering both the main road and the road leading to Burley on the Hill.

The mansion, Burley on the Hill, which has greatly influenced life in the village, was built for Daniel Finch, 2nd Earl of Nottingham, between the years 1674 and 1704. The Finch family bought the property from George Villiers, Duke of Buckingham.

King James I stopped there on his journey down from Scotland to ascend the English throne in 1603. King Charles I and Queen Henrietta Maria were entertained there and the magnificent festivities included the first performance of Ben Jonson's masque *The Gypsies*, William Shakespeare himself is believed to have appeared on stage in *Titus Andronicus* when it was performed by the London Actors (The Chamberlain's men) at Burley on the Hill on New Year's Day 1596, the performance being part of John Harrington's Christmas festivities.

Burley was once a thriving self-contained agricultural community, the chief employment being on the farms or at Burley on the Hill, which had a huge workforce both outdoors in the grounds, gardens, woods and carpenters' shops or indoors, for with 365 windows, even the window cleaner had a full time job! Now the village people work in nearby towns. The church of Holy Cross, which adjoins Burley on the Hill, was declared redundant in the 1980s, but the Council for Redundant Churches has provided funds for restoration work, so that it is hoped that four church services a year will in the future be held there.

The village school closed in the 1950s and the village shop and post office have also closed. The public house was once the parlour of Chestnut Farm, on the village green. In the last century the squire was determined to put a stop to the stablemen getting merry and fighting on their return from the bar parlour to their quarters near Burley on the Hill, so he closed the inn and had it moved to Hambleton where it still is today, known as the Finch's Arms. The squire had great power, as indeed had the vicar, who had the village pump moved from inside the vicarage gates to the village green, so that the vicar would not then hear the gossiping women as they came with their buckets for water! The pump remained on the green until mains water came to the village in 1962. Burley village green with its smithy was depicted on the advertisements for Cherry Blossom boot polish.

There is now no public village meeting place as the church room is used as a farm store. There are no council houses but new dwellings have been created from the disused workshops and stables at Burley on the Hill. Several new houses have been built along the Cottesmore Road.

Burrough on the Hill

Burrough on the Hill is near Burrough Hill Iron Age hill fort, which stands nearly 700 ft above sea level, on a marlstone escarpment, east of Leicester. There is evidence that the fort dates back to the 3rd century BC. Leicestershire County Council started managing Burrough Hill in 1970, opening it as a tourist attraction to the public.

The Grand National was held at Burrough Hill in 1873, but it is difficult now to imagine just where the race was run. In recent years a notable racehorse was bred at Burrough by Stan Riley, a local farmer, namely *Burrough Hill Lad*, trained by Jenny Pitman, which won the Cheltenham Gold Cup.

The Manor stands opposite the church of St Mary the Virgin, raised up in the centre of the village. The church seats about 100 people and has stood there for 700 years. The Manor was built in 1781, probably by Robert Peake. It belonged to Brasenose College, Oxford, until it was sold as a private house in 1941. It was beautifully restored in the late 1970s by its owners.

The old manor house of the Peake family stood at the south-west end of the village and was demolished in 1839 and the site renamed Old Hall Close. The foundations of the old house were discovered in 1948 when six prefabs were erected on the site.

By the early 20th century there were three large houses in the parish, which were used as hunting boxes.

Burrough Hill House, or Burrough Hall, was built in 1876 by C. W. Chaplain on the high ground to the north-east of the village, a stone mansion in the Tudor style surrounded by grounds, together with cottages for the workers. The second owner was Major A. Coates (the cotton family) who extended the building.

By 1900, Major W. A. Peake was living at Burrough House, a former farmhouse, near the village and lane to Owston. It was much extended with a large stable court and four worker's cottages built to the west.

The third large house was Burrough Court which stood about a mile from the village on the road to Twyford. Built in 1905 it later belonged to Marmaduke, Viscount Furness. Between the two world wars it became known as the meeting place for the hunting society of Melton, and in the autumn of 1930 was the site of the first meeting of Edward, Prince of Wales and Mrs Wallis Simpson. The Court also had stables and cottages to house the workers. The house, sadly, was burned down during the Second World War when it was requisitioned for troops. Burrough House and the Court are now part of Burrough Court Estate, farming about 2,500 acres of mainly arable land in the area. There is spectacular scenery around the village, which is a conservation area.

There are about 60 houses in the village itself. There is a village shop and post office which sells a variety of groceries and fresh fruit and vegetables. There is a pub, the Stag and Hounds, but no village hall.

Burton Lazars 🥀

'There is something uncommonly salubrious in the air here, as well as in the water which perhaps may increase its effects, situated as it is upon a gentle ascent, surrounded by high hills' – so wrote Nichols about Burton

Lazars in the 18th century. Indeed, today there is always a fresh breeze, and the springs in the village still flourish, although not used for drinking or medication any more.

Burton Lazars' claim to fame is that it was the site of one of the largest leper hospitals in England from 1160 to 1544. Some earth mounds remain, and several of the older houses in the village are believed to contain stones taken from the hospital site.

Burton Lazars once also boasted a racecourse used by the local hunts for point to point racing. The late Duke of Windsor, when Prince of Wales, was a regular visitor, as was his brother the Duke of Gloucester.

The village has changed very much, though the church still dominates the village from the highest point. A beautiful little church, it is well cared for by the members of the congregation.

The majority of the villagers do not work in the village. Its close proximity to Melton Mowbray has made it a popular choice for living in a rural situation, but with the benefits of a town. The village has been infilled with executive style houses and bungalows, but there has been no new building of small homes.

A village without a pub, the village hall is the centre of village life. The hall was opened in 1953 and is of wood construction.

The old school, now a private house, was built in 1836 by the squire, Edward Bouchier Hartopp, for 45 children. It had one large room, a kitchen, accommodation for the schoolmistress and a little cloakroom. There was also a windowless cupboard under the stairs where children were put if they misbehaved!

Burton Feast Day was always held on the first Sunday after St James' Day, 26th July. The tradition was that the village cricket team would play Great Dalby, and there would be roundabouts and swings and a beer tent for the men. That tradition was dropped during the Second World War. The Feast Day has been revived however, and now takes the form of a village fete organised by the church and other village organisations.

Burton on the Wolds

The Domesday Book in 1086 recorded Burton on the Wolds as Burtone. Today a main road runs through the centre of the village, carrying heavy loads to and from gypsum and coal mines which will continue into the 21st century.

Nonetheless, it is still a rural community of old and new. The oldest large house, originally the seat of Lord St Maur, is still named Burton Hall but since 1965 it has been a nursing home. The greater part of its grounds are now occupied by private property. The name of St Maur is perpetuated in a development of that name.

Research through gazetteers back to 1800 shows a fluctuating population and many trades long gone. A mill certainly existed in the last century but although in 1871 it is known that the miller was a William Wale, the location has long vanished.

The village school, rebuilt in 1908, had room for 140 pupils but its average was 98. The present modern school stands overlooking pleasant views off Barrow Road and has a considerably larger register, some from catchments in the area.

Both World Wars saw Burton on the map. The First World War saw Horse Leys Farm used as a landing strip for aircraft, with people coming from all around by cart and bicycle to witness the landings. During the Second World War, Wymeswold aerodrome was very busy, adjoining Burton. There was also a Polish displaced persons camp. Many of them settled in the area after the cessation of hostilities.

The original St Philip's church vanished without trace centuries ago, and extensive searches have revealed nothing. The little church used until the early 1970s is now part of a private house. The Wesleyan church built in 1846 remains active. During the last century the residents of Burton on the Wolds were assigned the south side of the nave of Prestwold church for their worship.

There have been various charities for residents of Burton, including an endowment for children from 1757 by Miles Newton and John Kirk, and bibles from the lord of the manor. The poor participated in the Packe and Cox charities, and the annual Feast day was the first Sunday after 12th August. All appear to have lapsed. During the Second World War, children at the village school received a voucher to assist in the purchase of shoes, usually at Christmas.

Caldecott 🦢

In ancient times the village was known as 'Cawcott' (where they're awk'ard). It lies in the beautiful Welland valley on the site of a Roman camp. It is situated between Rockingham Castle, the Seaton viaduct and the Eye Brook reservoir (built in 1937).

The ancient church and surrounding houses were built of local stone, in attractive patterns of warm browns and cream. The roofs were either thatched or tiled with Collyweston slate. The manor house stands at the top of 'Ducks Nest', now called Mill Lane. The old vicarage, now a riding school, stands on the outskirts of the village on the Uppingham Road, known as the 'Turnpike'. On that same road at the top of 'Gally Hill', so called because of a gallows that stood there, it is said that the noise of ghostly horses could be heard on certain moonlit nights.

Before the Second World War it was a self-sufficient village. John Bradley, the landlord of The White Hart Inn also made coffins, then he would put on his undertaker's hat for a funeral. There were three shops in the village. Mrs Birchnall of Monkey Puzzle House had a sign over the door saying 'Tea, Tobacco & Snuff'. The chief employment at that time was farming or the iron works at Corby, later to become the steel works, which eventually closed down, making many men redundant.

The village had a lively little school with excellent teachers. Children came to the school from the age of four to 14, the older children being taught in the 'big room' and the tiny tots in a small ante-room. There were roaring coal fires in the grates and oil lamps on dark winter days. Two asphalt playgrounds grazed knees in the summer and the two rows of outside lavatories were built over ash pits, the ashes being released on rising from the seats. When the wind was in a certain direction it was wise not to linger too long! The school was famous for its annual May Day with maypole dancing and the crowning of the May Queen on the green. The children became quite famous for their country dancing, singing and plays and it was a sad day when the school closed.

Castle Donington 🌿

Castle Donington is a rapidly expanding village in the north-west corner of Leicestershire, bordering the county of Derbyshire. Today, the main industries in and around the village include the East Midlands international airport, which was opened in the early 1960s and is located on the site of a Second World War bomber station, and a power station, which when opened in 1958 was the most advanced in Europe of its type. Light industry plays its part in employing many residents, concentrated mainly in the area of the new industrial estate, to the north of the village.

Past industries in the village consisted mainly of basket-making, the osier beds for which have now mostly disappeared under the site occupied by the power station. Framework knitting, lace making and a paper mill were also part of the local scene. Village men were also employed on the canal network and in agriculture.

Donington Park Race Circuit is known throughout the world. Prior to the Second World War it was the venue for the British Grand Prix. It hosts a full programme of motor car and motor cycle racing events throughout the season.

Castle Donington is an ancient village and dates back to pre-Norman times. The Domesday Book shows it as Dunitone. The castle, built in the 12th century, is no longer in existence as such. Only the double dry moat and fragments of the original building survive, but any visitor to the village would know where it once stood, Castle Hill and The Moat being the 'give-away' clues.

The main shopping area is situated in Borough Street alongside the 12th century parish church of St Edward, King and Martyr. The use of the church today is unusual in that it is shared by the Roman Catholic community, who hold services there. No burials have taken place in the churchyard since 1879. The gravestones have been laid flat, in family groups where possible, and only a few box tombs remain in-situ.

The village centre is given over annually to the revived May Day Market, when residents dress in medieval costumes. Another annual event is the 'Wakes', which are held in October by virtue of a charter granted in 1278, when the streets in the centre are again closed to traffic and used by the showmen. This is traditionally the time when friends and relatives of village people return to take part in the festivities and also attend the Harvest Festival, which is held on the same weekend.

An old village term, still in use today to denote newcomers to the village, is 'Eastwinders'. This term is believed to date back to the times when invaders from the Continent made use of the east wind to blow their boats across the North Sea and up the river Trent, which flows by the village at about one mile distant.

Donington Hall is a beautiful country house, set in ancient woodlands which are mentioned in the Domesday Book. There are still several very old oak trees in the park, many of which have a curious distorted appearance. It is believed this was caused by Selina, wife of Theophilus 9th Earl of Huntingdon, who owned the park at that time, topping out and selling the timber in order to build chapels in other parts of the country. The present house was erected by the first Marquis Hastings in 1795. The Hall is now owned by British Midland Airways and has largely been restored to its former greatness. The ancient herd of deer still roam, albeit with a lesser degree of freedom brought on by modern day use of the park.

Cold Newton 🐝

Cold Newton is situated about two miles from Tilton on the Hill, two miles north of Billesdon. Some 700 ft above sea level on the wolds, overlooking the broad and fertile Wreake valley, it is a small village in the parish of Loseby, with no church, public house or shop. Newton, spelt Niwetone, is recorded in the Domesday Book of 1086. Later the name changed to Newton Burdett when Hugo de Burdet became lord of the manor.

By the year 1799 the village had 15 families. The livelihood of the community was, and still is today, mixed farming. It is one of the few areas in Leicestershire where pigs can still be seen grazing in the fields. Ridges and hollows may be seen in some fields, this is where the lost village of Cold Newton once stood. It is now an ancient monument; the fields cannot be ploughed, only grazed.

The estates of Loseby and Quenby meet at Cold Newton. The famous Stilton cheese is said to have been first made at Quenby Hall by Lady Beaumont's housekeeper. Squire de Lisle, the present owner of Quenby Hall, gave a piece of land in the centre of Cold Newton to the village to commemorate Queen Elizabeth II's Silver Jubilee. The villagers then cleared the area and turned it into a village green.

Cold Overton 🐝

High on a ridge four miles north-west of Oakham, commanding a magnificent view of the Leicestershire and Rutland countryside, lies the village of Cold Overton, a mixture of mellow stone and brick houses and a church dating from the late 13th century. At 600 ft above sea level, they say that the winds blow straight from the Russian Steppes, hence the name Cold Overton.

Next to the church stands Cold Overton Hall, a Grade I listed house dating from the early 17th century, built for John St John, who was High Sheriff of Leicestershire in 1632. The Frewen Turner family occupied the hall from the late 17th to the late 19th century, when Lord John Manners lived there. One of his horses, *Seaman*, won the Grand National and is said to be buried in the grounds.

Until 1933 the roads to Langham and Knossington were 'gated'. Their removal necessitated roadside rail fencing. The material used for this was secondhand, originating from Newmarket, and most of this is still in use. The road through the village leads to Whissendine, and was still 'gated' until quite recently.

Until well into the 1920s bricks used for building in the village were produced in the local brickyard along the Langham Road. A private DC electricity supply for the village was generated from a building in the grounds of the Hall, the cables taken underground so as not to spoil the surroundings. There were also several lights along the village road. The tenants were allowed lighting but only one power point, and were charged for the supply. Water was pumped from a bore hole next to the rectory, initially by windmill and later by electricity. In 1946 the whole estate was split up and sold.

The Old Rectory dates from the late 16th century with 19th century additions. No rector has lived in the village since 1900, and the Church Commissioners sold the house in 1933 to Mr Montagu, who owned the rest of the village. During the Second World War the house was used as a hostel for conscientious objectors and later for twelve Land Army girls.

Stone House, an early 19th century house on the edge of the village, was built by John Frewen Turner as an orphanage for 20 girls, and is now a farm, run by the same family for the past 40 years.

The village has changed very little over the years. Some of the old cottages, said to have been thatched, have been pulled down, and only three dwellings have been built since the Second World War. Many houses no longer needed for estate workers and farmhands have been bought by professional people who commute to work in nearby towns, and also by retired people. There is a nursery on what was the site of the kitchen gardens for the Hall, and a post office, but no shops, although until the introduction of rationing during the war, the old post office used to sell sweets.

Coleorton 🦐

Motorists hurrying along from Leicester, Loughborough or Nottingham to Burton on Trent, Ashby-de-la-Zouch or Birmingham are barely aware that they have passed through Coleorton. From its early recorded history it has been described as a 'scattered village', and so it remains today. Although buildings have come and gone, there are very few alike. The church, school, post office and council houses are all at some distance from each other. The rolling fields give little indication of the industry carried on here for over 800 years, although the discerning eye might notice the undulations which denote subsidence and the blackness of the soil.

Coal mining goes back to at least the 13th century. Evidence of old pit heads is to be found in nearly every field. Where the coal was near the surface, workings were only a few feet in diameter and depth, and were known as 'bell pits'. Later workings were much bigger. Coleorton was an important mining centre in Elizabethan times, and in the late 16th century 10,000 tons a year were being moved out of the village by donkey carts.

The motorist may not notice the entrance to British Coal's regional headquarters at Coleorton Hall. However, generations of the Beaumont family lived here as lords of the manor, and were inextricably linked with the development of the coal industry locally.

Sir George Beaumont was instrumental in the development of the ill-fated 'Forest Line' canal from Thringstone to Loughborough, which was to be linked to Coleorton by rail. Unfortunately, less than a year after opening, in February 1799, the canal collapsed after a rapid thaw of heavy snow and was never reopened. In 1833 another Beaumont financed the Coleorton railway, which linked with George Stephenson's famous Swannington to Leicester line. The last pit in the village, known as 'Bug and Wink', was closed in 1933, when neighbouring New Lount opened.

Other industries flourished at different times, mainly associated with mining. The brickworks also provided bricks for St Pancras station in London. A popular footpath, known today as the 'Rope Walk', was where the cordwainer hung the ropes which were used by donkeys to haul coal to the surface in days past. Miners made baubles in their spare time, and their range of alabaster ornaments were sold far afield. Today it is the walker who sees traces of these past activities, and the village is now primarily an agricultural and residential area.

The Beaumont family have now moved away, but their legacy remains. The present hall, the third on the site, was built by the 7th Baronet, Sir George Beaumont in 1809. The parish church stands in the hall grounds, and has some traces of its medieval origin, although it suffered damage during the Civil War and was extensively restored again in the mid-19th century. The church school and the almshouses were rebuilt by the Beaumonts at that time also.

Sir George Beaumont not only gave practical support to the parish, but was a widely-known patron of the arts. William Wordsworth stayed at nearby Hall Farm with his sister Dorothy. While there, he wrote a poetic tribute to Sir Joshua Reynolds, which is inscribed on an urn erected by Sir

George in the hall grounds. A painting by John Constable, another visitor, of the urn in its lime grove setting is in the National Gallery in London. In 1823 Sir George gave his collection of paintings to the nation, thus stimulating the establishment of the National Gallery, a project he had cherished for many years.

Cossington ✣

The village is a mixture of old and modern buildings, with thatched roofs, Swithland slates and locally made bricks, several cruck cottages, stately homes and some attractive modern dwellings, catering for all walks of life. There is a thriving school, and the well known Old Mill Restaurant and two nurseries are popular locations.

The Old Rectory, now privately owned, dates back to the 16th century. The beautiful 13th century church, All Saints, has lovely stained glass windows, carved pews and screens and a pipe organ, presented by the Methodists of Sileby when the Wesleyan chapel closed. This is used and enjoyed by a lively congregation.

The village is served by a good Parish Council, who are arranging new street lighting in the village. In 1985 they revived an old custom, by renovating the old village pinfold, which in olden days had been used to impound straying animals, to be reclaimed by payment to the pinder. This is now a feature in the village with seat and garden, and is celebrated each year by midsummer revelry.

The village also had two benefactors who began the Platts and Babington Charities, now administered by trustees. The Platts Charity owns land which is rented to parishioners, and donations from the income are given to help the needy. In earlier days these were mostly farm workers living in the village, who were paid very little. They were given calico, winceyette, coal, bread and beef at Christmas time. Today, money is allotted to those on low incomes. The Babington Trust owns seven houses in the village, which are for needy villagers, and they also own some ground which is used as allotments. These rents are also used charitably.

The present manor house was built in the 1930s, on the site of the old one which was demolished. Lord Kitchener, of First World War fame, visited this family home, and his father's grave is in the churchyard.

Cossington Hall still stands serenely on the main street. Built by the Fisher family, it has been the setting, over the years, of many grand occasions. Now, although the Hall looks unchanged from the outside, it is divided into three individual dwellings. The grounds were sold separately, built on in the 1960s, and became Fisher Close.

Some old customs have died out. One, the blessing of the plough, was on a Sunday in January, followed by Plough Monday when villagers knocked on doors asking people to remember the plough and collecting money from householders. Rogation Sunday was also celebrated, when the rector, church officials and choir walked through the fields, blessing the crops. The Hudson name is no longer prominent in the village, but it could once be seen over the doors of the village shop, the public house, the blacksmith's and the wheelwright's. Now, sadly, it can only be seen in the churchyard.

War Memorial at Cossington

Coston 🥀

The village of Coston is situated seven miles east of Melton Mowbray.

Coston consists of 15 houses, one of which is a lodge occupied by MENCAP. Most of these houses were built in the late 1800s but there are two which are built of stone and are considerably older than this.

The population of the village is just over 30, this has been dramatically reduced since the year 1801 when it was 150.

There is a church which was in existence in the 13th century, additional parts of the church having been added later. In the church is a plaque to the actor by the name of Mr Temple E. Crozier, who was accidentally stabbed on the stage at the Novelty Theatre. Services are held twice a month, this being the only social event in the village.

Years ago there was a manor house, which was apparently in the possession of the Berkeleys at one time. The old bridge leading to this manor is all that remains.

There was also a vicarage which was finally demolished in the 1950s. In this vicarage was a parish room which was used for village functions such as whist drives etc.

At one time there were ten privately tenanted farms. Now there are three. There is a coach building firm which employs some 20 men.

At one time Coston had its own public house which was known as the Swan, this was situated opposite the church.

There is a ford in the village which attracts many a family on a warm sunny day so the small children can play in the water. Years ago there was a water mill near this spot.

Cotesbach 🥀

It is believed that there was a settlement here before the Romans came to Britain and built the Watling Street which skirts the village within a mile from the gibbet northward, now the A5. At that time the area was heavily wooded, probably with beech trees.

On the death of the Earl of Essex, beheaded by Queen Elizabeth in 1600, all his possessions were forfeited to the Crown. The land was subsequently sold off and Cotesbach bought by George Bennett, who built the manor house in 1630. The red bricks were made from clay found in the village. Bennett, the first lord of the manor to actually live here, continued to do so until the mid-17th century. There is a most interesting heavily studded door of great antiquity at the manor.

One of the most important events in the history of Cotesbach occurred in 1607 when 5,000 men, women and children from neighbouring counties gathered here to fill in ditches and level the walls and hedges which signified enclosure. This revolt was put down by the army before it could spread to other parts of Leicestershire. Before enclosure 30 families were recorded in the parish register; in 1626 only 18. Cotesbach today has 60 houses and a population of 130.

The church of St Mary the Virgin is flanked by its two cedar sentinels. In the churchyard miniature daffodils thrive, snowdrops, violets and cowslips are found and huge 400 year old yew trees spread their branches. The chancel dates back to the 14th century and although there has been a church on this site since about 1220, it has been partly rebuilt and extended. Recent removal of rendering has exposed an assortment of materials. In contrast to the hewn stone of the chancel, for parts of the north wall and tower, round stones, as found in a stream bed have been used and also red brick for the extension in 1812.

Opposite the church is Cotesbach Hall, built by Dr Edward Wells, rector 1701–1727 (a noted mathematician and theologian), on the site of the original Elizabethan rectory and used by rectors of Cotesbach until 1880.

There is an ash tree reputed to be 600–700 years old in the Hall garden, together with ancient yews and a 100 year old monkey puzzle tree.

The Hall has been in the Marriott family since 1759 when Rev Robert Marriott DD purchased the lordship of the manor and 1,100 acres. Being squarson (ie squire and parson) he lived at the then rectory from 1768 and the manor house became the farm house. Around 1790 some excellent farmhouses were built on the estate.

Notable members of this family include John Marriott, born here in 1780, who composed the well known hymn *Thou Whose Almighty Word*, published after his death.

Mrs Towers has seen many changes in the 32 years she has run the post office. Surely the tiniest post office in existence, being about 6 ft by 4 ft wide in the porch of her cottage.

One very important change for the village has been the opening of the bypass A426, which has returned Cotesbach to a quiet village again.

Countesthorpe 🦚

Surrounded by farmland, Countesthorpe occupies 1,213 acres. It is a large bustling village, six miles south of Leicester. Until the mid-1960s the growth of Countesthorpe was very slow, but from then until 1975 several large estates were built causing a rapid growth in the population. Further applications for housing development were rejected until 1988 as residents fought to maintain both their village identity and the surrounding green belt. Despite their efforts of over 10 years, permission was finally granted, and the population of 6,500 will increase once more.

The centre of the village contains most of the old buildings, the street plan having been laid out in 1767. There are examples of timber framed, Georgian, Victorian and Edwardian houses together with more recent styles. The parish church of St Andrew stands on the site of a Saxon place of worship, and was originally started in 1220. It was restored in 1841 and again in1907, but only the 14th century tower remains. The village also has a Baptist chapel, erected in 1863, a Methodist chapel (1845) and a cemetery (1893). On the gravestones in the churchyard and the cemetery are recorded the names of long-established Countesthorpe families, like Chapman, Gillam, Lord, Ringrose, Herbert, Wale, Burley and Tompkin.

Although originally a farming community, the cottage industry of stocking knitting started at the beginning of the 18th century. At its peak, there were over 20 frame knitting shops, but now only a few are left. One is used as premises for making handbags, another by a printing firm. So knitwear and light industry, as well as farming and the retail trade still provide some local employment. Until recently Countesthorpe could also offer fresh bread baked on the premises, and a delivery of milk from a local farm, but both these businesses have been forced to close because of the pressures of modern trading. Today the bakery is a restaurant.

Another building now used for light industry was once the village school. Situated on the corner of Foston Road, it was built in 1884 by a non-religious board. The Church school was originally housed in the upper storey of the church room, adjacent to the church. It was first built in 1753, then made into a single-storey school for 60 children in 1841.

Also in 1884, to the west of the village, the Cottage Homes were opened by the Leicester Board of Guardians. These were intended to house orphan children so they could be brought up in a home environment instead of institutions. There were eleven cottages, the superintendent's residence, an infirmary, isolation block, schools, workshops and a

52

swimming bath. For many years, the homes were very successful as a self-sufficient community but it became obvious that the children were isolated from village life and were moved away to more suitable accommodation. Many of the houses were boarded up by the early 1970s, and some occupied by squatters. They are now listed buildings, most being privately owned and used as family houses. Others are used as a base for young people's activities, a nursery school, music lessons, and a YTS scheme.

One of the events which takes place every year on the first Saturday in June is the Scout Gala. This fundraising effort can be traced back to the beginning of the century when the village residents got together to raise funds for the Leicester Infirmary. The Cottage Homes Band led the fancy dress parade round the village, and the Hospital Fête in the afternoon was a grand affair, attracting people from other local villages. According to tradition, one of the farmers used to stand one of his pigs on the wall to watch the band go by!

Croft

Mention this village's name to the more mature of Leicestershire folk and their eyes will take on a dreamy look. 'Oh yes', they sigh, 'Sunday school outings to Croft Hill, picnics and fun when we were young'.

There it stands today, dominating the Soar plain – a solid granite eminence, not always the scene of sunlight and children's laughter. The great of the land, including the King, Queen and Archbishop of Canterbury, gathered there in AD 836 to put their crosses to a charter granting land to a monastery in Worcester. Three hundred years later no less than 44 men were hanged there, their bodies 'More pecked of birds than fruit on garden wall'.

Also on the Hill, above where St Michael's church now stands, there were built, in ancient times, little eminences called 'Shepherds Tables' where at certain times of the year shepherds had a day of festivity.

Prior to the Norman Conquest, the village was known as Crebre or Creg, then Crafte. Not until the 16th century does the name Crofte or Croft appear. .

In contrast to the Hill, at its foot is the Hole, or rather the southernmost granite quarry in England, which was officially opened in 1868 by Henry Davies Pochin, although granite slabs from Croft were used on the Fosse Way. Granite sets and curbs were made by the men who were not actively engaged in agriculture, the clickety-clack of their hammers being heard all over the village. Farmers complained that the quarry blasting scattered stones all over the fields injuring their sheep and cattle, so the quarry bought the land and thus the complaints ceased. Croft granite is found all over the world, nowadays mainly crushed for roadbuilding.

The late 19th century red syenite church of St Michael has only one Norman window and a Norman font as reminders of its past. It stands halfway up Croft Hill while the little, lovingly cared for, chapel is now almost in the quarry.

The Hill has always 'belonged' to the villagers and successful attempts were made to stop its enclosure by lords of the manor.

The Crofters had always grazed their sheep and cows there and had caught rabbits and hares. The fight for the Hill still goes on as the Hole gets bigger load by load.

Farms still surround Croft, for the village has not grown much although its proximity to the motorway network has made it a commuter village. There are two small developments at either end and several light industries flourish. With its own primary school, community centre, not to mention its thriving Silver Band, Croft is certainly one of the friendliest and liveliest of Leicestershire villages.

Cropston

Cropston is situated four and a half miles north-west of Leicester on the edge of the Charnwood Forest. The village is a hamlet of the parish of Thurcaston about a mile away and the parish church of All Saints is there. The earliest written record of Cropston is in 1299 when it was held by one Richard Le Waleis. In 1781 an area of about 360 acres was enclosed and became known as Cropston Fields, later Cropston Chapelry.

Cropston reservoir and its pumping station were built in 1866, flooding around 200 acres. It was built by Irish navvies, and seeing an opportunity, a Mr Billy Booten set up a shed near the then manor house to supply them with food and drink. This was known to the Irishmen as 'the Shant'. When later the manor became the Reservoir Hotel, the nickname 'The Shant' was remembered and stuck, and is still used locally.

The other inn, the Bradgate Arms, is more typically the 'village pub', and with its skittle alley and cricket field behind is a centre of village activity. It is over 400 years old, and for 100 years until quite recently, the Jackson family were landlords. The last Mr Jackson to be there remembers the elderly ladies coming in the evenings to fill their white jugs with beer – and having a quick half and a good gossip at the same time! Also after evening milking time milk was sold at twopence halfpenny a pint fresh from the herd of cows kept in a field behind the pub. So, if you took your jug to the Bradgate Arms, you could have it filled with either milk or beer!

In 1801 there were only 22 villagers' houses, and 100 years later there were still only about 30; today there are more than 400. But, conversely, there has been a loss of the old village shops – the bakery-cum-dairy, the greengrocer, dress shop, the butcher's (with its own slaughterhouse) have all gone, leaving just a small post office and a garage.

With the parish church being at Thurcaston, the chapel, the Evangelist Free Church built in 1850, was an important centre of village life, both for its church services and social occasions. All the children went to Sunday school, and the anniversary celebrations, with the building packed for the choir singing and later the sports and games for the children – at which all the children got a prize – is a well-remembered highlight of the village year. The chapel is still well used for activities.

The other great event in the Cropston social calendar was the annual Fancy Dress Ball at Thurcaston, at which the Earl and Countess of Lanesborough judged the costumes. This was run by Cropston Cricket Club, whose Annual Dinner (gents only, two and six pence) at the Bradgate Arms must be another memory to cherish! The club still plays on a field behind the pub, and is of a high standard.

There was a well-remembered umpire who could always be relied upon to give a batsman out as opening time approached!

Croxton Kerrial 🦌

This Leicestershire village is situated on the A607, seven miles from Grantham and nine miles from Melton Mowbray. The village is built on a west facing hillside, with spectacular views over the Vale of Belvoir.

It is understood that the name Croxton (pronounced Crowston) dates from the 7th century. The name Kerrial was added later and marks the influence of the Criel, Cryall or Kirrel family.

There is evidence of a Bronze Age settlement in the area, as there are extensive burial barrows connected with 'King Lud's Entrenchments' (an ancient monument now part of a nature reserve). These formed part of the local boundaries of that age. There are also traces of a Roman settlement to the west of the present village.

There are 114 houses in the parish today. The Local Authority built four dwellings in the 1920s and 30 dwellings between 1945 and 1965. The rest of the houses belonged to the Duke of Rutland. In recent years houses from both sectors have been sold for private ownership. The traditional building material is local ironstone with slate, or in years gone by thatched, roofs.

The village now has one inn, one grocer, one butcher, one carpenter/ furniture restorer, one florist, a post office and six farms (all of which are owned by the Duke of Rutland and rented to the tenant farmers).

The local church of St John the Baptist is mainly 15th century. The interior has 42 pre-Reformation benches with very ornate woodcarvings on the ends, said to be the largest collection in Leicestershire. They were thought to have originally come from Croxton Kerrial Abbey.

The abbey was built in the 12th century. It was situated in the park about one mile south-west of the village. It owned extensive estates throughout the East Midlands, and played an important role in the wool trade with Florence. It had a dominant role in village life until the Dissolution of the Monasteries by Henry VIII. The abbey was then demolished and the land bought by the first Earl of Rutland in 1543. He used it as a hunting seat. (It is now owned by the present Duke.) The Belvoir Hunt is still very active in the area to this day, although the hounds are now kept at the kennels in the grounds of Belvoir Castle. There was also a racecourse established in the park grounds early in the 19th century, but no longer used for this purpose. The three large fishponds are still to be found, and are fed by natural springs.

Two features of the village are the continually running waterspout on the edge of the village, which is fed by the springs from the fields behind and the Horse Pond, used by travellers when calling at the Peacock Inn opposite.

Every year there are May Day celebrations, and another event that is held in the village is the Ascension Day Bible Presentation. Bibles are presented to children leaving the village school to go to Bottesford. The money for the Bibles comes from the wills of Edward Hallam (1683) and William Chester (1703).

Another charity is the Ann Parnham Charity. On the 14th January 1837, she left the sum of £250 to be invested, the interest to be used to maintain her gravestone and to be distributed amongst the widows of the parish on St Thomas' Day (21st December). A further sum of £150 was to be used to educate seven poor children of the parish. This is now paid to the school.

Desford ✒

The village of Desford lies about eight miles due west of Leicester and despite its name is situated on a hill at an altitude of about 400 ft above sea level. It belongs to the Duchy of Lancaster.

Until the Industrial Revolution the village was a wholly agricultural community and there are many references to yeomen and husbandmen in the parish registers, which are virtually complete from 1559 onwards. In the first part of the 19th century Desford became an industrial village, with many framework knitters but the population then fell and only rose again towards the end of the century with the opening of the South West Leicestershire coalfield. Today with post-war council and private housing estates it is a village of some 3,000 to 4,000 inhabitants, many of whom commute to Leicester, Hinckley or neighbouring towns for work. It is fortunate, however, in having two large industrial employers within the parish, although outside the village, and there is still one working farm in the middle of the village, although there were three in the 1960s.

When the old manor house, a fine Georgian building, was demolished in 1959, remains of Roman kilns were found on the site. An Elizabethan rule-measure was discovered under the floorboards in a house of Elizabethan date which is now a bank. In the 18th century and early 19th century the church must have had its own band since a large serpent (an old wind instrument) from Desford is preserved in the Newarke Houses Museum in Leicester, where can also be seen 19th century shop fittings from a Desford grocer.

A number of interesting and historic buildings survive in Desford including the church of St Martin and Old Manor Farm, an early brick built farmhouse of about 1640 of which the original survey survives. This was owned by the Muxloe family in the 17th century and is the site of one of the few apparitions recorded in the village. It is said that a Muxloe went to the Welsh wars and there met a beautiful Welsh girl who spoke no English. He put her across his saddle and brought her home to be his wife. Here, among strangers, she pined and died, and is said to wander still, dressed in a shawl and a high Welsh hat.

The inhabitants of Desford have a reputation for being independent – some might say awkward – and an incident in 1932 reached the National Press. When water from the village well opposite the Miners Institute was declared unfit for human consumption the pump handle and bucket were removed by the authorities. Several villagers, annoyed by this action, drove lorries and cars to Market Bosworth and marched up to the

Council offices shouting 'We want our pump'. They came back to Desford triumphant with the handle and bucket and both items are thought to be still in the village somewhere.

Today the framework knitters and the miners have gone, though the latter are commemorated by the installation on a site in the village of half a winding wheel from Desford pit which was organised through the good offices of a flourishing Desford Local History Society. The old Board School of 1876 is now the local Scout hut and its later, separate, extension is now the church hall. The inhabitants are fortunate, however, in having within the village a modern primary school and, on a separate site, Bosworth College which is both a 14–18 years school and Community College.

Diseworth 🦢

During the Second World War there was an airstrip in north-west Leicestershire known as RAF Diseworth, named such after the nearest village. Later when it was developed as a civil airport it was probably felt that Diseworth was too modest and obscure to lend its name to such a venture, and so it was known first as Castle Donington airport and later, of course, East Midlands. So although the airport plays a prominent part in the life of Diseworth today, it seems slightly detached from it. This is helped by the village lying in a hollow, away from the flight path.

Some airline and airport employees have chosen to live in Diseworth. Most of the other residents now find their employment well outside the village and commute to Derby, Loughborough and Nottingham. In the past the village was more inward looking and had its own industries. There have been at least three brickyards, using local red clay. These supplied the surrounding area, and much of Loughborough is said to be built with Diseworth bricks. Local rumour has it that many of the houses in Long Whatton were built with bricks that fell from the carts going to Loughborough. Other occupations included frame-knitting, and the seaming of stockings and gloves. One children's singing game had the rhyme:

'From Long Whatton – never let it be forgotten
Comes old Isaac Adkin's rotten seaming cotton'

Isaac Adkin was a local carter in the 19th century and the rhyme suggests that he brought the hosiery to Diseworth for stitching.

The principal industry, however, was agriculture and its dependent activities. Many of the surrounding fields show evidence of the ridges and furrows of the open field system in use before the land was enclosed in 1797. Today, farming is still an important part of village life. There are several farms within the village and others on the edge. There is still a blacksmith, and a joiner descended from the wheelwright who was essential to farming. The village still has a general store with a post office, but the cobbler, baker, tailor, ironmonger, butcher and coal merchant who served it until recently are no longer here. The nine pubs which were known are now reduced to two.

As in most places, the changes that have occurred in the last 50 years have been dramatic compared with the slow development of the previous centuries. There is thought to have been a Roman settlement here close to where there are signs of an ancient ford crossing the brook. It is believed that Diseworth was on an ancient route crossing the Trent valley. Later when the Vikings ousted the Saxons and occupied parts of the Midlands they appear to have taken over Diseworth. The principal roads presumably date from this period. They are Hall Gate, Lady Gate, Clements Gate and Grimes Gate. Gate is a corruption of the Danish word 'gata' meaning 'street'. One of the families in the village, the Jarroms, are believed to have been living here since Viking times.

William Lilly was born in Diseworth in 1602. He was the son of a prosperous farmer who later became famous in London as an astrologer. His birthplace in the centre of the village has become a place of pilgrimage to some modern astrologers who hold his work in high esteem.

The parish church, dedicated to St Michael and All Angels, stands in the middle of the village, its broach spire noticeable from most of the approach roads. It incorporates Saxon work in the chancel and is a modest well-kept building that is in tune with the community it serves. The Baptist church also plays a prominent role in the life of the village. The present building in Lady Gate dates from 1773, but for 20 years before that meetings were held in an upper room at Lilly's Cottage. At about the same time Methodism found a following in Diseworth. The present church in Hall Gate was built in 1887.

The records and burial grounds of the churches show many of the same surnames occurring again and again, while representatives of some of these families are living in the village today. There are occasional complaints that today the place is not very exciting, but that is all part of its character. Even when, in 1957, it had the distinction of being the epicentre of an earthquake, only one casualty was reported – a bag of flour which fell off the shelf in the grocer's shop!

Dunton Bassett 🌿

Dunton Bassett is midway between Leicester and Rugby on the A426, some 1,300 acres in size. Mentioned in the Domesday Book, there is strong evidence to suggest that a settlement existed in Saxon times and perhaps earlier still. Humps and hollows in Old Hall Close, near to the 13th century church, are all that remain of the foundations of Old Hall, an ancient mansion.

Agriculture has played an important part in the life of the village, changing its emphasis according to the needs of the time. Reflecting modern day changes, there is now only one working farm, with more and more of the land put down to grass.

Houses reflect a good architectural mix, from the 16th, 17th and 18th centuries to Victorian and modern building styles. There are twelve listed buildings, including the parish church.

According to White's Directory, in 1846 there were 553 inhabitants, many of whom were framework knitters, reflecting the importance of this new industry. As well as farming and allied craftsmen, other occupations included bakery, butchery, bricklaying, plumbing, shoemaking and tailoring. There were three public houses.

A survey in 1986, undertaken by the local History Group, records 288 residences and approximately 714 people living within the parish. Very few of these are employed in the village, the majority of those in work commuting daily to follow wide and various occupations – only three are now employed in the hosiery and knitwear industry. There are still three public houses, two of which were mentioned in the 1846 directory. There is a flourishing school, post office and village store.

Dunton Bassett school's origins are unusual in that it was never a 'church school'. It was founded in 1849 by a Mr Thomas Stokes, a wealthy hosier of Leicester and lord of the manor of Dunton. He gave the land, built the school, and endowed it with the Stokes' Charity, which continues to be paid to this day, not, as originally used, to help the poorer children to continue their education and to pay the schoolmaster, but for extras such as school outings.

The village being on a hill, the church spire is visible for miles around, and a benchmark on the south-west corner of the porch indicates that its height (480 feet) is marked on the Ordnance Survey map. The main building is 800 years old, for about the year 1200, the lady of the manor, Geva, began its building. Her likeness in a stone carving may be seen above the south vestry doorway. Geva's daughter Maud married one Sir Richard Bassett – hence the second part of the village's name.

A busy village hall sits at the bottom of the hill in the middle of the village. Built and donated to the village in 1895 by the late Orson Wright, a well known builder who later built the Grand Hotel in Leicester. He gave the hall in memory of his parents who were natives of the village. The hall has always been the hub of the social life in the village and since the demolition of the Methodist chapel is now the only available secular meeting place. It serves also, during school terms, as an additional schoolroom and assembly hall for the local primary school.

The village has a notable, though until recently little known historical connection with the Twigden family. They were resident in the village in the late 19th century, living in what is now the post office and being a fairground family in the summer. The Twigdens have the distinction of operating one of the first roundabouts in Britain and took the first mechanical ride to operate at the Nottingham Goose Fair. In the 'off' season they stored and renovated their machines in various parts of the village, and took part in village Wakes celebrations by giving free rides to the village children.

Earl Shilton

Earl Shilton is approximately four miles from Hinckley and eight from Leicester. The name Shilton came from the Old English for a settlement on a ridge. The prefix Earl was added after the Conquest in 1066 when the village was held by the Earls of Leicester. There was a castle near where the church now stands, but nothing remains of it. There is just a mock ruin to indicate its position.

It is proposed to bypass the village in the early 1990s but at the moment the A47, the very busy main road from Leicester to Hinckley goes through the village. This road seems to change its name quite often but the centre is always known as 'the Hollow'. One of the streets is still called Station Road although the railway never actually came to the village and the nearest station is now Hinckley. There are two street names which might seem odd to visitors. Kings Walk is nothing to do with royalty but is named after a man called King who used to walk there; and Doctors Fields is so named because a local doctor used to prescribe walks in the fields instead of medicine; the name remains, although the fields are all now built on.

In 1778 an enclosure act was passed for 'dividing, allotting and enclosing in the Lordship of Earl Shilton, several open fields, meadows and commons, and in particular a large common called Shilton Heath, containing together about 1,500 acres'. This open heath was a favourite place for horse racing in the 18th century. At the time of the enclosure Thomas Lord Viscount Wentworth was described as the patron of the rectory of Kirkby Mallory, of which Earl Shilton was still a part. At that time the church was dedicated to St Peter, but in 1855–6 when the village became a separate parish it was rebuilt, except for the tower, and was then dedicated to Saint Simon and Saint Jude. Its inside walls and chancel roof were painted at the expense (and some also say by) the rector, who was helped by the children of the village.

In 1800 the village contained 249 inhabited houses and eight uninhabited. At that time a windmill was built, the amount of £800 being raised by subscription. This mill was damaged by lightning in 1902 but continued to work until 1917 when it was again damaged by a storm. This time it was not repaired. The building survived until about 1940 when the site was quarried. Quarrying for granite is no longer carried out but the shoe and hosiery industries are still located in the village and new light industry is coming in.

Elmesthorpe ✿

When travelling from Hinckley to Earl Shilton the picturesque medieval church of St Mary can be seen silhouetted against the horizon. It is a lovely little church, partly ruined, but this seems to add to its charm. The tower is 17th century and the font 12th or 13th century. It is set in a beautiful award winning churchyard, with lovely views across to Burbage Common and woods.

From here you can look down to the site of the old village, originally Aylmersthorpe, which was to the east of the bridle path. In 1297 it was a flourishing community of 40 to 50 families with several farms. However, due to a failing economy and the plague, Aylmersthorpe became depopulated and has now disappeared. Thus, on the night before the battle of Bosworth in 1485, King Richard's army was unable to find accommodation, and the officers sheltered in the church, the soldiers camping outside.

Church Farm was built in 1710 for a Mr Storer, who kept it as a public house for several years, being in an ideal situation for travellers on the main Market Bosworth to Lutterworth road. At that time approximately 40 people resided at Elmesthorpe. The farm's most famous owner was a trader and farmer called Richard Fowke, who issued the only farmer's wage token known, a halfpenny, of which only 18 were struck. One was

found in recent times and sold for £520. An avid historian, he owned a splendid museum.

A pleasant tree-lined walk along Station Road brings you to the 'new' village. This came into existence when a railway station was built here in 1863. Lady Noel Byron (Baroness Wentworth) improved the land by drainage and new roads were constructed. The Earl of Lovelace commissioned a well known architect, Mr C. F. A. Vosey, to design a row of six workers' cottages and an inn to accommodate travellers. The busy station had a weighbridge, and workers walked from outlying villages to catch the train. Behind the inn, pony racing took place, an important event with competitors travelling from as far afield as North Wales. More houses were built and in the 1920s a small boot and shoe factory opened here.

During the 1930s the government devised a scheme to bring families from depressed areas to make a living on the land. In 1935 the Land Settlement Association purchased Church Farm as accommodation for the manager and offices, packing sheds were erected and they built 43 smallholdings with greenhouses and several houses for staff. Practically overnight the population increased dramatically. Many families settled to a farming existence, though sadly some returned 'home' or found other employment. The empty smallholdings were then let to young families with agricultural experience. Elmesthorpe became well known for its market garden produce.

In the 1960s the station closed, the factory moved away and the LSA decided to close Elmesthorpe. Some tenants purchased their 'holdings', while a few moved to other estates. The land was kept for agriculture and the vacant houses eagerly purchased, modernised and enlarged, and, thanks to the efforts of new and old residents a splendid community centre replaced the dilapidated 'hut'.

The 1986 census showed a population of 513 and present day Elmesthorpe consists of a church, inn, private school (formerly Church Farm), community centre, several farms, a few smallholdings, a nursery and kennels. There are no shops and just one private bus per day, but it is an attractive, rural and very friendly village.

Empingham

The village of Empingham in Rutland is built on a south-facing slope rising from the north bank of the small river Gwash. People have been living in this fertile valley for thousands of years. Bronze and Iron Age tools and jewellery, foundations of Roman buildings and roads and a large Saxon cemetery containing 135 graves, have been found within the parish. Empingham was probably the settlement of the Saxon Epping tribe. The manors of Empingham and Normanton were held by the Normanvilles in the 12th and 13th centuries. They built the early part of the parish church of St Peter, and the chapel at the east end of the village, dedicated to St Botolph. In 1284 a grant was obtained from King Edward I to hold a market in Empingham on Thursday weekly, and a fair every year 'upon the eve, day and morrow of St Botolph; viz 17 May'.

From this time, only three families spanned over 600 years as lords of the manor: the Basynges for about 150 years, the Mackworths 300 years and the Heathcotes (later Earls of Ancaster) 200 years. Each family served as MPs and Sheriffs of Rutland. Henry Mackworth seems not to have taken sides when, during the Wars of the Roses, on 12th March 1470, the battle of Losecote Field was fought across the northern part of Empingham parish. It is reported that about 10,000 men were killed, and part of Empingham Wood is still called The Bloody Oaks.

All the farms are now owned and worked by the farmers and their families. Some smaller farms have been joined to others and the farmhouses and cottages sold. Most of the farmhouses and older buildings in the village are built of limestone with Collyweston slate or thatched roofs. Some are built of brick as the Ancaster estate had its own brick kilns. Several groups of fine stone barns have been converted into attractive houses.

Empingham has been on the bus route between Oakham and Stamford since 1927. There are two shops selling groceries and greengroceries, one also an off licence and newsagent, and the other the post office. Two shops sell antiques, and the Primrose Hall stores bicycles for sale. Up to the early 1930s, out of a population of 550, all the workers and tradesmen were connected with the land, and few worked outside the village. There was a wheelwright, saddler, blacksmith and farrier, carpenter, cobbler, carrier and coalman, thatcher, thresher, shepherd, milkman, baker, a butcher slaughtering his own beasts and a general store and post office. Today only the general store, the post office and the milkman remain.

The village hall, called the Audit Hall, was a large barn used by the Ancaster estate agent to audit the farm accounts. In 1937 it was given to the village by the last Earl of Ancaster, together with a collection of old armour and weaponry, displayed around its walls. Opposite the Audit Hall is a thriving public house called The White Horse Inn.

There are no longer May Day celebrations organised by the school, or Dodgy White's fun fair in the White Horse Inn yard during the church's

St Peter's Feast week, or Rogation Sunday beating the bounds, or Plough Monday, or the Sick and Dividing Club Supper, or the 2/6d Invitation Dances in the Audit Hall as in the past. Now part of the parish is under water. Rutland Water, originally called Empingham reservoir, is on the western doorstep. It offers fishing, sailing, rambling and picnic areas for thousands of people from near and far.

Enderby

Enderby lies four miles south-west of Leicester on the north-west tip of the Soar valley, above the flooding levels.

The village stands between two main roads out of Leicester and in recent years two motorways, the M1 and M69, have been constructed with access only a mile and a half from Enderby on the old A46 Coventry road. Here large industrial developments are taking place. The village itself has resisted large scale development except for a housing estate bordering on Narborough parish and now in Enderby parish under the new parish boundaries.

Centuries ago, the quarries became a major industry and in the early 18th century the stocking frame came to the village. By 1844 there were 350, but the cottage industry of framework knitting became depressed and the picture one gets of the 19th century village is of very poor, ill-fed and overworked people, with a lack of care and attention by the church. One curious fact emerges that there was no vicarage after about 1640 until 1867 and this caused a long run of absentee vicars. The church grew dark, damp and neglected. At the same time, nonconformity grew rapidly and the Congregational chapel was built in 1822 occupying the highest position in Enderby, followed by the Methodist chapel in Cross Street, 1849. In 1868 Charles Brook completely rebuilt the church and a vicarage. Then the church took its proper place in the life of the village.

Charles Brook is also remembered as a squire of Enderby Hall, situated in Hall Walk a short way from the church. He enlarged the school known as the Church School and his statue still stands in the old playground. This school was used as an arts centre after the modern school was built in Mill Lane and opened in 1958 by Sir William Brockington, now known as Brockington College.

Enderby has six hostelries – the most picturesque being the thatched New Inn situated in the High Street, part of the old village. In Cross Street stands the very old Nags Head where an old custom called the 'Selling of the Wether' took place on Whit Monday. The 'wether' was a meadow given by John of Gaunt to the men of Ratby to be auctioned each year for the hay and became an Enderby tradition. The bidders smoked long clay pipes as they gathered around the table, the bidding taking place as a coin was passed from hand to hand. Permission to cross the meadow had to be obtained from the current year's owner until the council made an order for a right of way and the tradition became another memory of the past.

The Co-operative Society, then 'Enderby Co-op' figured largely in Enderby village life for many years. They had their own farms, slaughter-house, bakery, dairy and three or four grocery shops in the village. An impressive emporium was built by the far-seeing Mr Gittens, on the corner of Co-operation Street, where anything from ladies and gents' fashions to haberdashery could be obtained. Also in King Street was the Co-operative Boot & Shoe factory providing employment for the local people for a long period. Part of this is now Enderby Civic Centre used for Parish Council meetings and various activities. The shopping area is also around this centre and there is a busy post office, chemist and newsagents among others. The 'Co-op' is now a modern superstore. The bank is operated in the oldest cottages of Enderby and has recently been re-thatched.

The quarries have ceased to operate and have become the scene of land-filling operations.

Fleckney 🍃

Fleckney, tucked away between the A6 and the A50, was, and still is one of the chief industrial villages in South Leicestershire.

The Domesday Book records 'Flechenie' as being smaller than nearby Saddington or Wistow, but it expanded over the centuries, and today it is still growing with a population of almost 4,000.

The village is built on glacial clay, and this provided the opportunity for brickmaking. The village pond was a claypit, and samples of the local bricks can still be found in the Lamp Lighter's Hut in The Parade. Now ducks, not bricks, are the pond's main attraction.

Hosiery soon followed, Fleckney being the home of some of the first hand-built frames, and some years later the well known firm of Wolsey Ltd had its humble beginnings here. Today Wolsey Lane and Wolsey Close are reminders of times past. Other names from the past, such as Wranglands, Mosswithy, Long Grey, Dribdale and Bratmyr, old field names taken from an 18th century map, have been used as street names on the new housing estates that have developed since the 1970s.

Most of Fleckney's industry is today confined to a purpose built estate, where there is hosiery and various other trades, including plastics and engineering. These provide work for many local people, particularly the womenfolk, but the majority of Fleckney's working population commute to work. One other village industry worthy of mention is Furnivals Mineral Works, founded in 1897 and based on the local spring water. It was, and still is referred to as 'The Pop Shop' factory.

The church of St Nicholas dates back to the 12th century, but can boast neither tower nor spire, and only two, not very tuneful bells. There are also two chapels in the village.

Abraham Deacon, born in 1828, was perhaps one of Fleckney's best known sons. He was the founder of the Carmel Baptist chapel. Through his marriage he gave the village a resident chemist, Miss F. E. Potter, who was the first woman apothecary in the country.

In 1841 Fleckney was described as 'a pretty little village', and in 1926 as 'a dull manufacturing village'. Today it can no longer be called 'little' or 'dull' but the original combination of industry in the countryside still prevails, and that age old friendly greeting of, 'hullo me duck, 'ow are yer,' will hopefully, still be heard in the streets of Fleckney for many years to come.

Foxton

One villager can still picture Foxton as it was at the turn of the century – 'Another dawn on another spring day – the maid is up preparing to light the kitchen range fire at the Lodge, a farm labourer walks across the yard to the cowshed to start milking, the baker's apprentice lifts out the final batch of loaves from the oven.

'We hear the cock crow – our day is beginning, fires to light, water to fetch from the pump. The hens and the pig will need feeding – the children do this before running up Middle Street to the school. The village schoolmistress notes that attendance is reduced owing to illness and the stormy weather.

'The older boys have joined their fathers in the brickyard, on the Incline Plane building site, in the fields between Foxton and Gumley, at Mr Spriggs' ketchup factory. In all the cottages, scrubbing floors and cooking dinners, women think of their daughters in service in Leicester and Market Harborough. Mothering Sunday was just two days ago and the bunches of primroses are as fresh as when first picked.

'Milk, coal, sharpened knives and pins are being sold from house to house. Mothers and young children are waiting to be served in the shops – Mr Brown weighing out potatoes, Mr Hurst wrapping up a new pair of boots, Mr Tebbatt selling stamps.

'Several horses are waiting to be shod outside the blacksmith's – young lads are trying to creep nearer the fire to warm up on this raw, cold day.

'The carrier for Harborough is going up the hill past the Black Horse pub, now being rebuilt. The tree planted for the old Queen's jubilee is well established just opposite the church entrance.

'Lunchtime – men in the fields take out their bread and cheese and bottle of ale; children come home from school and are late back for the afternoon lessons; more work needs doing in the house – ironing all the clothes washed yesterday – a warm job even in this weather.

'The afternoon has fled by and everyone starts returning home ready for dinner. Families join in a sing-song round the piano or play cards with friends and relations. The children are outside playing in the barn – never hearing the first call for bed. People attending the chapel's classes in shorthand are poring over their books.

'The clock strikes nine o'clock – we climb the stairs to bed at the close of another day.'

Frisby on the Wreake

Frisby on the Wreake lies four miles south-west of Melton Mowbray. Mentioned in the Domesday Book as Frisbi, then Frisby super Wrethek, the village's population was steady at around 400 for many centuries, increasing to around 600 since the 1970s with the new housing development in Hall Orchard.

The parish was enclosed in 1760 when the tithes were commuted. The 400 year old tithe barn at Gables Farm is the oldest building in the village apart from the church, which was built between 1200–1500 and is dedicated to St Thomas of Canterbury. Much of the interior woodwork has been lovingly carved by local craftsmen. During the latter half of the 18th century, the Rev William Brecknock Wragge gave the parish a Gretna Green reputation by marrying anyone who arrived at the church door, with or without the banns being read.

In the village is an ancient stone cross with ornamental mouldings standing on three steps, and at Frisby Hags (top road) is another smaller shaft on four circular steps commonly called Stump Cross. The Main Street remains virtually unchanged since it was the main highway between Leicester and Melton Mowbray. The Old Black Horse at the top of the main street was a coaching inn from those bygone days and must have lost a lot of trade when the turnpike road was opened in 1810. It remained an inn until 1974 and is fondly remembered as a cosy 'spit and sawdust' type hostelry. The existing pub, The Bell, dates from 1759 and has in recent years undergone extensive refurbishments, becoming the social centre of the village.

Until the mid-19th century, Frisby was served by the Wreake Navigation which in the main followed the course of the river. Its popularity waned with the advent of the railway in 1846 and the locks soon fell into disrepair. The Wreake is now a popular spot for fishermen and the old gravel workings nearby are home to abundant waterfowl and the Melton Sailing Club.

Zion House (1725), one of the few remaining thatched properties in Frisby, was formerly an 'Academy for Young Gentlemen'. It is said that the master and his pupils were not early risers and one morning a couplet was seen chalked on the shutters of the window.

'Cheer up my friends. Pray do not weep.
We are not dead but fast asleep.'

There is a tiny cottage attached which is reputed to have been the home of George Davenport, the notorious highwayman who was hanged at Red Hill, Birstall in 1797. Rumour has it that on foggy nights, a phantom coach and horses can be seen coming across from Brooksby down the Rotherby Lane into the village.

In the past the village was self-supporting, having numerous shops and traders including blacksmiths, butchers, miller, baker, carpenters, shoemakers and tailors. Today, there are two general stores, one of which also serves as a post office. Frisby still has its plumbers, builders and other individuals carrying on their businesses within the village, which all helps to retain the village community. At the turn of the century, Holwell Works at Asfordby Hill employed many Frisby men who walked the three miles there and back daily to work. Today, the majority of Frisby's inhabitants commute to Leicester, Melton, Loughborough or Nottingham.

Gaddesby

Gaddesby is built on an ancient, south-facing site above a brook, seven miles south-west of Melton Mowbray. There is evidence that there was a motte and bailey castle at the top of the hill, probably built during the 12th century civil war period of Stephen and Matilda.

The present Gaddesby Hall was built in the early 18th century. No one family has occupied it for any length of time, but its most famous owners were the Cheney family after whom the village pub is named. During the Second World War the Hall was occupied by British and American troops, and stories are still told in the village of the bus loads of girls who would come out from Leicester at the weekend.

There were numerous springs in the village and two village pumps can still be seen in Chapel Lane. On the corner of Chapel Lane and Cross Street is a large boulder (probably a glacial erratic from the Ice Age) known locally as 'the blue stone', from which John Wesley is known to have preached when visiting friends in the village.

St Luke's, one of the finest village churches in Leicestershire, was built between the mid-13th and 14th centuries of limestone and ironstone.

Monument to Colonel Cheney in Gaddesby church

70

There are three monuments in the church, one to William Darby and his wife, dated 1498, one to an unknown knight of around 1500 and one (thought by many to be somewhat incongruous) to Colonel Cheney. This latter, sculpted in alabaster by Joseph Gott in 1848, depicts Colonel Cheney at the battle of Waterloo on one of the four horses reputedly shot from under him, while below, on the base of the monument, a panel depicts Colonel Cheney in hand-to-hand combat with a French officer trying to recapture a lost Napoleonic eagle. The horse's teeth have been stained by the apple placed in its mouth each year at harvest festival time. This monument once stood in a conservatory at Gaddesby Hall, but it was moved to the church on rollers when the estate was sold in 1917.

The first known school in Gaddesby was held in the church in the south-west aisle, until the new schoolroom was built in 1868. It is said that D. H. Lawrence had a lady friend who taught there and that he visited the village with her.

The older houses in the village were built to house workers at the Hall or as hunting lodges. Names such as Old Forge Cottage and Wheelwright's Cottage indicate the past history of the buildings, and a number of them are listed buildings, including an old windmill just outside the village.

A handful of old families remain in the village and there are those who remember a time when all but two of the men in the village were employed locally. However, the village still retains a pleasant rural character due mainly to its old brick houses, herring-bone brick walls, thatched cottages, ancient yew hedges and mature cedar trees (popularly supposed to be descendants of those planted by the Crusaders).

Gaulby

As a village Gaulby lays no claim to beauty nor to fame; no rows of picturesque thatched houses, no great Manor or Hall. The church, founded in the 11th century, has no visible remains of its early foundation but it is a village where people have lived and worshipped for over a thousand years. It lies hidden and unknown in the East Leicestershire uplands; like many similar villages it is of Danish origin, probably older as Roman potsherds and Saxon jewellery have been found in the area.

The earliest reference to Gaulby (sometimes spelled Galbi or Galby) is in the Domesday Book. It has always been an agricultural hamlet and even today the only employment is farming. There is no shop, post office or pub. The church is the only institution to maintain village life, providing a focus and meeting place for all who live here.

The 20th century brought change to Gaulby, from a rural farming community to a satellite village of Leicester with new modern houses whose occupants commute to work. Some of the old houses and cottages do remain and it is said by past inhabitants of one of them that there is a ghost there as 'things' have been heard or sensed in the early mornings about four o'clock, slow measured steps going up the main staircase.

Gilmorton ᘓᕤ

The village of Gilmorton is mentioned in the Domesday Book, when the manor belonged to Robert de Veci.

The present Victorian church is in a very poor state of repair and is in danger of being closed. It replaced a 'dilapidated Early English structure' when built in 1861. The church is mainly notable for the large amount of stained glass by Kemp of London.

The school was founded by Mr Edward Chandler in 1774; at that time he was Master of the Worshipful Company of Joiners. He provided a schoolhouse and dwelling houses for a schoolmaster and a schoolmistress. The master was to be paid £10 a year for the education of 20 poor children, but he could add to this by taking private pupils. The school is now in the Old Rectory and the original school is now part of the Crown Inn.

Gilmorton always has been and still is an agricultural village. There are still several working farms within the village. At the end of the 19th century there was a thriving cottage industry in knitting and older members of the community remember their parents telling them of three or four people getting together and renting a cottage in order to work there on their frames. There was a small knitting factory in one of the old cottages. Today Gilmorton is a commuter village. However, there is still one cottage industry as model soldiers are made in the outbuildings of one cottage.

Older villagers note the passing of public transport with regret. There were buses to Rugby, Lutterworth and Leicester and one could always cycle to Ashby Magna to catch the train to Leicester. Now it is essential to have a car. Public transport appears to have been a problem before, as the building now used as a post office and general store was built as a Railway Hotel. Unfortunately the railway never came!

In the past Gilmorton was well provided with shops and tradesmen. There were bakeries, butchers, a cobbler, two blacksmiths and at various times, numerous general shops. Now, there is a post office and general store, a butcher and the Village Stores, which has won the Leicestershire award for the Best Village Shop.

Close to Gilmorton on the road to Ashby Magna, there is a bend in the road known as Jingle Bells Corner. There have been many accidents here as cars end up in the ditch, failing to negotiate the corner. Some of these accidents are reported to have been caused by the sight of a ghostly carriage emerging from the spinney.

Glen Parva 🦋

Taking the road to Lutterworth from Leicester, Glen Parva is reached after passing through Aylestone.

The parish is now mainly a residential area with some light industry. The housing development began after the First World War along the principal roads and, although halted for the duration of the Second World War, continued through the post-war years by infilling along side roads. More recently, a number of local nurseries and market gardens have been sold off and housing estates built, remembering past gardeners with the road names, eg Featherby Drive, Parsons Drive and Bradshaw Avenue. The population is approximately 6,000.

Archaeological digs have been carried out on the surrounding site and evidence of Bronze Age, Roman, Saxon and medieval settlements have been found. The grave of a Saxon princess was found in the area in 1868. She now rests in the Jewry Wall Museum in Leicester, a model of her beside her bones. Buried with her were the tools and jewellery she would need in the next world and nearby, two soldiers to guard her.

The manor house, a lovely black and white timbered building, is now an hotel. After a fire in 1850, a Roman well was found when rebuilding work was taking place.

Kitty's Brook, which runs into the river Sence, is now culverted for the majority of its way, but years ago, Kitty, a white mare, used to appear on moonlit nights to warn of forthcoming danger to anyone who saw her.

In 1793, the Grand Union Canal was extended from Aylestone passing through the parish and on to Blaby, enabling the brickworks to develop. The canal is still a pleasant place to take a stroll and a haven for wildlife. A walk has now been developed using the old Great Central railway line and the canal towpath. A hundred years elapsed between the building of the canal and the coming of the railway.

The floodlands by the river are now under threat of gravel extraction.

The Manor at Glen Parva

There are plans to landscape the area after extraction with lakes and islands for leisure activities and nature reserves.

Glen Parva is rather unusual in that it has no church. It also has had a chequered history by gaining and losing parts of its area in successive local government and ecclesiastical boundary changes. These changes brought close association with Aylestone, South Wigston (in particular the home of the former Leicestershire Regiment – the Tigers – in Glen Parva Barracks) and Lubbesthorpe. There is now growing community interest in the area as newcomers are welcomed into the parish.

Glenfield 🪶

Glenfield is a large village built on an incline sloping down from the Leicester boundary to the Glenfield Brook. The original settlement was established before AD 800 not far from the old Leicester Forest, near a hunting lodge called Bird's Nest Lodge.

There has been a church in Glenfield since the 11th century. The present church was consecrated in 1877 and the ruins of the previous building can be seen in the churchyard. An old statue transferred from the old church is believed to be of Lady Joan de Glenfield.

The first chapel for Methodism, built on Station Road in 1821 was replaced in 1876, by a new and larger one; the land having been given by the man after whom Ellistown was named, E. S. Ellis Esq, a wealthy coal merchant and chairman of the Midland Railway Company. The Ellis family was friendly with Robert Stephenson, who as son of the great George, engineered the making of Glenfield Tunnel on the Leicester–Swannington line in 1832. The tunnel is 1 mile 36 yards long. The railway closed in 1965 but the tunnel is still there. The entrance is covered, but the embankments remain landscaped into the surroundings.

There are a few Georgian houses and cottages and the Old Rectory, now a hotel, has a Georgian front built onto a yeoman's house of an older period. It has a Tudor staircase and a spiral staircase that goes up to the roof. Backing onto the brook is a stone cottage which was a Quaker meeting house with a burial ground behind it. Nearby is Oakley's Farm, the only one left in Glenfield.

In 1851 there were 544 people living in 113 houses in Glenfield. Most of the employment was in agriculture and framework knitting and there was much poverty during the 19th century. After the First World War, land in the Liberty Road and Sports Road area could be bought for 6d a square yard. A benefactor gave large plots for poorer people to use as smallholdings. The owner of a bacon factory gave them packing cases to build huts, and they transported them tied onto bicycles. As soon as they had one room completed, the family moved in. They were known as Bacon Box Houses. Gradually permanent houses replaced them, all with very long gardens.

Up to the 1950s, a true Romany encampment with decorative caravans was a familiar sight. Since the Second World War the land of every farm in Glenfield, except one, has been used for housing. All the land of Sir Samuel Faire was built on and his house was demolished and modern units were made to accommodate children of Barnardo's Homes. County Hall stands on the estate of another large house.

Back in the 1950s the villagers united to resist efforts to include Glenfield in the Leicester boundary, so now, despite having a population of 10,000, Glenfield is still a village.

Glooston ꙮ

Glooston is a small village built on the Roman road Via-Devana, now known as the Gartree Road. On various occasions Roman remains have been found in the surrounding fields to remind occupants of their predecessors. The village now has a population of 43, mainly pensioners and people who travel to work in the nearby towns. Today only one house is occupied by a herdsman, whereas in 1900 almost all the cottages were occupied by labourers working for the four milk producing farms in the village. Today only one farm remains as a milk producer, the others concentrating on arable and stock.

Boasting only a church and an inn, villagers have to travel to Market Harborough some eight miles away for their shopping. Until the late 1970s travelling salesmen including a butcher, baker, grocer, green-grocer, fishman, clothier, and hardware merchant called on the villagers weekly or fortnightly. Now the only deliveries made are the daily papers, milk and a freezer van which calls once a fortnight.

Glooston church was built in 1220 and was rebuilt in 1866. Contained in the church is an embroidered sampler worked by a ten year old schoolgirl from the village school in 1879. The school at this time was in one of the cottages in Adelphi Row.

Great Glen 🦋

Great Glen, otherwise known as Glen Magna, got its name from its position lying in a valley where the river Sence crosses the A6 just south of Leicester.

The principal buildings are the church of St Cuthbert, Early English with some stonework remaining from the original Saxon church and with a Norman porch, the Georgian Methodist chapel and several big houses.

Before the Second World War Great Glen had a population of about 500 who earned their living as farm workers, on the railway or in hosiery, most of the latter at Rowleys in Fleckney. There was at one time a small glove/hosiery factory in the village. The building was later the Band Hut, where the village band held their practices under their bandmaster Mr Grain, who was also manager of the Co-op, the village shop. Later still this building was used as a dinner centre where the village school children had their mid-day meal. It was finally demolished to make way for Brookfield, sheltered homes for the village elderly.

Pastimes were mostly rural; gardening for the men on one of the two allotments, skittles, cricket and football, and for the young folk, dancing on Saturday evenings at Brandrick's. The WI played a big part in the women's lives. For the children the chapel Sunday school outing was an event much looked forward to. For entertainment the village band gave a

'Sacred Concert' every Sunday evening on the green, handy for the musicians to nip across the road to the Greyhound to 'wet their whistles' afterwards.

The highlight of the year was the annual carnival and fancy dress parade. The parade through the streets was always headed by the village band, Mr Pink Hubbard wearing his leopard skin and proudly beating the big drum. The carnival has long been superseded by the Great Glen Gymkhana.

In those days there was a village cobbler, Mr Bodicote, sitting at his last with the tiny nails held between his lips and a pyramid of shoes on the floor behind him. For new shoes, Cavey Bill came out on the bus from Leicester every Wednesday with a suitcase full of samples, calling house to house. Mr Drury from Burton Overy brought his fish and chip van to stand outside the Corn Stores. There didn't seem to be anything you couldn't buy in the village, and all delivered to your street if not your door – bread, meat, greengrocery, hardware, even drapery from Peter Shipp's van.

Greetham

Greetham (meaning enclosure or settlement on gravel) is a pleasant village with a population of about 450 people, once part of Rutland. It is situated six miles from Oakham.

The village is a mixture of stone cottages, several thatched cottages, converted barns and modern detached houses. It is mainly a farming community, but there are a few business people commuting to the nearby towns and cities, plus RAF personnel from the neighbouring Tornado base at Cottesmore.

There is the 14th century church of St Mary, which in 1985 was struck by a freak thunderstorm which sent masonry flying and the weather vane from the steeple crashing to the ground.

Not far from the church is the protected site of the ancient manor house where Edward II was reputed to have stayed. The rest of the site has recently been developed into a housing estate.

The villagers are especially proud of their community centre opened in 1981, which was built from money collected through fund raising events, Sports Council and local government grants. It caters for most sporting and social events and serves as a meeting place for young and old alike.

There are three public houses, a well stocked village shop, post office, garage, garden centre and stone quarry. Two cottage industries, one making old fashioned rocking horses, and another making gifts and presents provide employment for local people.

A building next to the post office is of historical interest. Around 1861 a well known stonemason, Mr Halliday, who at that time employed 47 men and four boys, used to insert pieces of carved stone into his workshop wall which he had collected on his travels, the result of which is very unusual.

One old custom which has died out is 'Plough Monday', when the menfolk of the village used to dress up in masks or blackened faces and drag a plough around the village collecting money.

There is a saying 'Grievous Greetham where they pine 'em'. One explanation is said to be that the vicar of the parish was so badly paid that he starved, and another that things were grievous because the villagers were so poor!

Griffydam

Although Griffydam doesn't appear on all road maps, it really does exist! Situated on the A447 and only seven miles from East Midlands Airport.

The name of Griffydam was said to come from the legend that a griffin, which was a fabulous creature with the head and wings of an eagle and the body of a lion, roamed the village, terrorising the villagers and trying to keep everyone from the only source of water. The well still exists, although no longer used. However, it has been proved by a local historian that the name is of Scandinavian origin and came from the words 'Gryfja Damnr', meaning a cleft or valley with a dam or stream.

The village is known to have been in existence for several centuries. Some of the old industries were a pottery and a brickworks, but the oldest known industry was wool making. One of the lanes is called The Tentas and is on a hillside. This is where the wool makers were said to have erected tent-like apparatus on which to dry the wool and the sheepskins. As in the old days, farming is to some extent still quite active, but many mineworkers lived in the village and worked at the now extinct New Lount Colliery which lay in the village of Newbold, Coleorton, which lies about half a mile to the west of Griffydam.

Griffydam has two chapels, the Methodist and the Wesleyan Reform which are still in use today. The Methodist chapel is one of the oldest chapels still in existence and was built in 1778. It was recorded in the Methodist magazine of 1825 that John Wesley held a service in Griffydam in 1743, even before the chapel itself was built. The *Methodist*

Recorder told the story of what happened. 'A squire who had great influence among the colliers resolved, if possible, to hinder the preaching. John Massey, an athlete, a renowned pugilist, the terror of every wake and fair in north Leicestershire was appointed captain of the anti-Methodist gang . . . No doubt the little evangelist was quite well aware of the plot against him but he never showed the white feather and seemed rather to enjoy a spice of danger. Calmly he proceeded with song and prayer.' Wesley cast such a spell that John Massey was completely won over. The converted collier became one of the most successful local preachers in the neighbourhood. John Massey was buried at Griffydam in 1819, aged 87 years.

Apart from the chapels there were four public houses, only two of which still remain. Gone is the Rising Sun and the Griffin, which lay only 50 yards from the Methodist chapel. The two remaining are the Waggon & Horses and the Travellers Rest, which has been transformed into a night club.

Groby

The original part of Groby is historically interesting. It is mentioned in the Domesday Book of 1086, when it had a population of about 80. Numbers grew slowly reaching 250 in 1800, then nearly 1,000 in 1920. Since then the population has grown tremendously.

There are quite a number of interesting houses, one of the most important being Bradgate House off the Markfield Road. This was built about 1854 by the Earl of Stamford. He owned the whole of Groby and the villagers had to use his mill in which to grind their corn. He built St Philip's and St James' church in 1845 as the road to the parish church at Ratby was so rutted his carriage was liable to overturn. He also built the village school in 1873, the children previously having been taught in a cottage. This cottage is now called The Old School House, 57 Leicester Road.

Another building, the Old Hall, is historically famous. It was built in the 1400s on the remains of a Norman castle. This must have been very large as when the church was built adjoining it, remains of its ovens were unearthed. One of the occupants of the Old Hall was Elizabeth Woodville, who married King Edward IV. Her two sons were the Princes who were later murdered in the Tower. The Old Hall is now a farmhouse and very well maintained.

In 1925 the Earl of Stamford sold part of the estate. The sale took place in the Bell Hotel in Leicester and villagers were able to buy their cottages if they wished. Up to this time no new houses had been built in Groby but this situation was altered by builders buying plots of land. They slowly opened up the village and now in these later years Groby has more than quadrupled in size and has become a commuter village.

In former times the only occupation for men was in the granite quarries, the Victoria Stone Company and on the few farms. The wives' only opportunity of earning money was taking work from the woollen firms at Ratby and Anstey. This work was fitting feet onto stocking legs. It was done on a machine called a 'Griswold' in their homes and it was quite common to hear the clacking noise these machines made as one passed by. A cottage still stands in Chapel Hill where knitting frames were made. The frames can now be seen in the Newarke Houses Museum, Leicester.

In the last 30 years or so Groby has developed considerably. There are now four modern schools and a Community College which adds much to the cultural life of the village. There is also an industrial estate and various shops in which many local residents are employed.

Gumley 🦎

Travel approximately eleven miles south-east from Leicester and you arrive at the village of Gumley, perched high on a small range of hills.

The present 110 inhabitants mainly live on either side of its one and only street, at the top of which stands the church of St Helen, built in the grounds of Gumley Hall. The Hall, now unfortunately demolished, was built in 1764 and in 1946 was rented for two years by Group Captain Leonard Cheshire, VC as an experiment in community living for ex-servicemen and their families. The gardens and lake were laid out by Capability Brown. All that now remains is the clock tower, built in the style of an Italian campanile, and the weathercock.

Colonel G. A. Murray-Smith and his ancestors figure large in the past and present of Gumley, the family buying Gumley Hall in 1897 and owning buildings and land known as Gumley Estate. He is the president of the flourishing cricket club, owning the land upon which the pitch and pavilion stand. In the cricket season travellers through the village may best remember their visit by being held up until the 'end of the over', as the Gumley to Laughton road cuts through the cricket pitch.

In the past the usual work was either farming or in service at Gumley Hall. Today many villagers now travel to their chosen occupations.

80

Farming, however, is not forgotten as there still remain three farming families within the village, as well as stables.

Come rain or shine, walkers, suitably dressed, trek along the street of Gumley taking in the fresh country air, or they follow the many field footpaths in and around the village – but beware after dark: Gumley possesses no street lighting.

When the wind blows from the east, it is easy to believe the saying that there is nothing between Gumley and Siberia.

Gumley wasn't always without a shop, as nearly 100 years ago the Weston-Jesson family obtained a house and built onto it a shop and slaughterhouse, where the process of rearing, killing and selling meat was carried out until 1932. These premises are now occupied by the granddaughter of John Weston-Jesson and her husband who, after restoring them, opened them to the public where butchering implements, farm tools and machinery of a bygone age can be seen. The village once also boasted a baker's and post office, but these have long since gone.

The population in 1821 was 289 with many children and so, in 1864 a school was built, but by 1933 it finally closed its doors as a place of education, only to be used as a village hall. By the sheer determination of villagers money was raised to build a new hall, the old school premises being demolished in the late 1960s.

Hallaton 🦡

Hallaton is a small, picturesque village lying on the borders of the Welland valley in the south-east of the county, with a population of just over 400. The oldest place of interest is Castle Hill, a short distance to the west, with its well preserved motte and bailey. Traces of Roman habitation have been found, and evidence of iron ore, and it is believed that ironstone from this site was used to build the church of St Michael and All Angels which dominates this side of the village, with its broached spire and fine octagonal pinnacle. Dating from Norman times, the bulk of the present church was built in the 14th century. A unique feature is the chime which plays the tune 'Old Dunsmore' four times every twelve hours.

A cluster of houses, mainly thatched, surrounds a small green, where the war memorial and conical stone butter cross can be seen. From here the High Street, packed with houses and cottages of varying size and fabrics, winds gently upwards, leading to another, much larger, green and duck pond situated at the northern end.

Today it is difficult to believe that Hallaton was once a thriving market town, and probably the centre of economic life in the eastern half of the county. It appears as Heleton in the Domesday Book, a small agricultural community. But in 1224 Henry III granted a weekly market on Thursdays. By 1284 Hallaton was a split manor, Bardolph and Engaine, which were each granted similar markets, and twice yearly fairs in June and October. Another three day fair at Ascension was allowed in 1304. Cattle from Wales and other parts of England were driven here for fattening in the rich fertile pastures of the Welland valley, and horse fairs were held regularly.

By the beginning of the 19th century the population of Market Harborough, eight miles away, a medieval 'new town', situated on one of the country's main north/south highways (now the A6), had overtaken Hallaton. Gradually the markets died out, and the last horse fair by 1863. Only the butter cross and street names, such as Hog and Horn, remind us of its busy past.

A railway branch line, opened in December 1879, increased the population, which reached 775 in 1891, and it remained a self-supporting community well into the 20th century. Every trade necessary for the life of an agricultural village was represented, and although today only one shop (including the post office) remains, the school, built in 1888, and the chapel, built in 1822, are still thriving.

The village is best known for the bottle kicking and Hare-Pie Scrambling which take place every Easter Monday. The bottle kicking is a game without rules, played between Hallaton and its neighbouring village Medbourne. Its origin is uncertain, but is probably connected with ancient boundary disputes of ancient 'kingdoms'. The hare pie, baked locally and distributed by the rector before the 'game' begins, is also thought to have ancient origins. However, when the Enclosure Act took place in 1770 a piece of land known as Hare Crop Leys was given to the rector for his use, on condition that he provided a 'Hare Pie, a quantity of Ale, and 2 dozen penny loaves to be scrambled for after Divine Service on Easter Monday'. Today, the event attracts many people from beyond the two villages and is in no danger of dying out.

Harby 🌿

The settlement of 'Herdebi' is mentioned in the Domesday Book of 1086 and over 900 years later the present Harby is a thriving community, the largest village in the Vale of Belvoir. The north-western boundary of Harby is formed by the Nottingham-Grantham Canal. Built in the 1790s the canal was of utmost importance, bringing coal to the village and taking agricultural produce to the towns. The wharves, mill and brewery provided much needed work before the advent of the railway in the vale in the 1880s. Today the canal towpath gives hours of pleasure to walkers and birdwatchers, and impassable sections of the canal are being cleared by the Grantham Canal Society.

St Mary's church was built in 1485 in the Perpendicular style, although the chancel dates from the 14th century. The living is under the patronage of the Duke of Rutland who lives in nearby Belvoir Castle. Before the church was built it is thought that Augustinian monks from Croxton Kerrial Abbey held outdoor services at the village cross near the site of the present church. The remains of the original ancient cross were incorporated into the war memorial following the First World War. The craftsman who carried out this work sealed a small document of life in Harby into the memorial.

The population has remained fairly constant since the last century, but in recent years commuters and industrial workers have outnumbered farm workers as farming practices have changed and mechanisation has increased. The wheelwright, blacksmith, bootmaker, miller, baker, wharfinger, draper and dressmaker are occupations which are no longer found in Harby.

Many names in the village can be traced back through several generations, and names such as Watson, Boyer and Starbuck can be found in use today as street and house names.

Timber, mud and wattle were used for building and some older buildings retain these materials, and mud walls can be seen in the village. Local brickyards supplied materials for many of the cottages and the more precious ironstone was used for the most prestigious dwellings in Harby. Exchange Row is a terrace of brick cottages built by the Great Northern Railway 'in exchange for' farmworkers' cottages built of mud.

The school built in 1860 has been carefully extended, but the small belfry and school bell have been removed as they were unsafe.

The Second World War brought changes to the village skyline as an airfield was developed at nearby Langar. Many tall trees were felled and

Harby windmill

the top storey and sails of Harby windmill had to be removed as they obstructed the flightpath of the aircraft.

Any history of Leicestershire villages cannot be complete without reference to Stilton cheese. In summer months when milk was plentiful farmers' wives made cheese with surplus milk; the farmers then formed village co-operatives which were eventually taken over by large dairies. Some Leicestershire villagers still have a dairy in cheese production but the milk is now delivered by bulk tanker to the cheese factories. Harby's Stilton factory provides employment for a number of villagers and tours around the factory are available for visitors.

Hathern 🌿

Hathern is a working village on the A6 three miles north of Lough-borough, first recorded in the Domesday Book of 1086.

A clue that the village may have been Anglo-Saxon comes from the old carved font in the parish church of St Peter and St Paul, a 14th century

84

building of Charnwood Forest stone, much altered and rebuilt in the 19th century.

A 14th century cross stands at the centre of the village made up of Charnwood Forest stone and sandstone blocks. The shaft broke during a gale in 1916, but was repaired in the 1920s. It may have been weakened by the practice of local lads at the turn of the century of making bonfires on the top.

John Heathcoat, inventor of a lace machine, was apprenticed in Hathern, and educated at one time by the Parish Clerk. Heathcoat installed these machines in a factory in Loughborough and prospered until the Luddites smashed 55 of them on 28th June 1816. He then took the remaining machines, his Hathern bride, and some of his workmen to Tiverton in Devon.

In 1871 there were 1,120 persons in the village, about two thirds of whom were connected with framework knitting. The frames were usually operated by the men, known as stockingers, in their own homes or outbuildings (stockinger's shops) and many of these shops are still in existence throughout the village. The stockings were invariably seamed together by the women. Today high quality hosiery is still made by the third generation of a family business.

Hathern Band was formed well over a hundred years ago. At one time there were two bands and numerous choirs in the village. The present band, extremely popular and talented, wins many contests.

Residents of the village, when telling people they hail from Hathern, face the reply 'Oh, Wicked Hathern.' Why? No one really knows. But in letters written by the rector of Hathern, he refers to the Loughborough Magistrate of 1801–2 who said that Hathern was the wickedest place in all the world. Another magistrate later said he believed Hathern was a place given over bodily to the Devil!

Football and cricket have played a big part in village life. The first recorded cricket match between Hathern and Shepshed was in 1814.

Heather 🌿

Heather is set in north-west Leicestershire, entered in the Domesday Book of 1086, under its archaic name of Hadre. In 1189, Heather was given to the Knights Hospitallers of St John of Jerusalem – a religious order serving the sick and poor pilgrims. The church, which occupies the highest point of the village, is dedicated to St John the Baptist and lists rectors dating back to 1220. By this time the village was known as Hether. Today it is renowned for its unusual pronunciation of 'Heether'.

Unfortunately an idyllic English village lifestyle is a pleasure of the past, when everyone knew everyone else. It is highlighted for those who remember a pony and trap on Main Street, when it looked more like a quiet country lane, with its quaint cottages. Far removed from the thundering of heavy lorries today, taking a short cut to nearby motorways, towns and cities – the greatest bugbear to weekday life in Heather. Apart from the traffic aspect, changes to Main Street over many years are few. The small primary school, built in 1845, is today considered to be a vital asset. Also situated in Main Street are two village pubs, The Queens Head and The Crown Inn, the latter having parts dating from 1560. They continue to be the heart of village social activity. The prestigious manor house, next to the church, rebuilt in brick in 1731, is believed to occupy the site of a former preceptory.

Gradual expansion of the village came with the introduction of a general water supply in 1937, and mains electricity in 1940–42. These had been preceded by individual wells, oil lamps and candles. A turning point, whereby the gains were significant in bringing about sophisticated village life, although there are a number of people who feel a sense of loss along the way.

St Pancras station, London, a familiar destination for some village commuters, was built in 1865 with local Heather bricks. Village lads, only 13 years old, were employed to carry four of these bricks at a time from the kilns to the railway tracks. In 1900, these lads were paid a half crown for working 60 hours per week. Alternative employment for the average lad was farmwork or coalmining at this time. Occupations for girls were few. Most went into domestic service, working long hours for 10 shillings a month. However, opportunities today are endless, and Heather contains an ever increasing number of self-employed and small business people, content to earn a living in the local community.

Hemington

Hemington is a village in the parish of Lockington. Situated one mile south-east from Castle Donington, it occupies a low site at the foot of the hills between Lockington and Castle Donington. One feature of the village is the brook which runs beside the main road. In the past the brook has been known to flood, the worst in living memory being the flood of 1929, when the water was so high it poured between the cottages and drowned several pigs.

On the hills overlooking the village are traces of earthworks, thrown up during the Civil War for the purpose of an attack on Hemington Hall, then the residence of Sir John Harpur.

In the early 19th century the principal landowner was Sir George Crewe, Bart, who held the lordship of the manor. Some of the village is still in the hands of the Harpur-Crewe estate (which includes Calke Abbey, now a National Trust property).

The fishpond and the Hall have survived the centuries but the old church has nearly vanished. The church, built in the 13th century with an octagonal spire, has been in ruins for 300 years or more. As long ago as 1590 a visitor, Henry Wyrley, reported 'the glass was all ruined and the church not in use'. During the late 19th century the chancel was for years the abode of a mentally afflicted old woman who lived in a rough hovel of her own making, until the authorities condemned it for human habitation and took her off to the workhouse. The shell of the 50 ft high tower stood the test of time for around 700 years and suddenly collapsed into a huge pile of rubble after the heavy rains of spring 1986.

The New Connection Methodist chapel was built in 1797 but has recently been converted into a dwelling house. It stands next to the Jolly Sailor public house, which was originally a beer house.

Opposite Hemington Hall is the village green on which stands the war memorial. Nearby is the public house, the Three Horse Shoes. Horse drawn drays and later charabanc parties of miners from the Derbyshire coalfields would come to the Three Horse Shoes for their annual outings.

There are six thatched dwellings in the village, two of them being cruck cottages. One has been pebble dashed, but the medieval cruck cottage which has been well preserved and is still occupied, in the past housed a bakery which delivered bread to Hemington, Lockington and Kegworth. Since then it has been a post office and is now known as Post Office Farm.

The building alongside the Hall, known as the Nunnery, was used for many years as a barn, but has recently been converted to a dwelling house. It is believed that in past years, the nuns walking across a field to Castle Donington gave the field the name of Ladies Close.

Higham-on-the-Hill 🦐

The name Higham-on-the-Hill is derived from 'High Ham', a farm or manor above the surrounding country, though this is not shown in the Domesday Book. Rhymes said to originate in Higham bring in villages from the area. 'Higham-on-the-Hill, Stoke in the vale, Wykin for the buttermilk, Hinckley for the ale'.

Dedicated to St Peter, the parish church has the only complete Norman tower in South Leicestershire. The fine peal of bells include the Armada bell, cast by Thomas Newcombe of Leicester in 1589. The advowson was in the hands of the Fisher family, five of whom have been rectors in Higham. Most notable was Dr Geoffrey Francis Fisher. Later made Archbishop of Canterbury, he officiated at the coronation in 1953 of HRH Queen Elizabeth II.

Robert Burton, author of *The Anatomy of Melancholy* was born at Lindley Hall in 1577. He had a brother who gave an account of what he termed an 'accident'. An inhabitant of Higham moved a 'great Stone' lying in Watling Street, revealing 250 silver pieces bearing the head of Henry III, a gold ring set with a ruby, another with an agate and a silver ring! The Hall eventually fell into decay and was demolished during the Second World War to make way for an aerodrome, which was decommissioned after the war. The land is now used by the Motor Industry Research Association as a proving ground.

The late Jack Clarke quoted the following rhyme.

'Old Jack Brown is a funny fellow,
Old Tom Jaques keeps the key of the cellar.
Old Jack Knight he carries the news,
Old Bill Bott he mends the shoes.
Old Tommy Hollier rides in his gig,
Old Polly Woodburn keeps a fat pig.'

Old Jack Brown was an eccentric and decided to build a house, carrying all the bricks in a handcart from Wilnecote approximately ten miles away. The iron windows he carried on his back from Birmingham, a return journey of 42 miles for each frame. They were tough in those days! Fourteen years later the house still needed a roof, which the parish paid for; but poor old Jack never lived in the house. There were two back and front doors and two staircases. This building has now been converted, and is owned and used by the Methodist church.

Agriculture was the main occupation in the 19th century, though there were bakers, a wheelwright, a miller, carpenters, shoemakers, a blacksmith and a tailor. A typically self-sufficient community, the men grew vegetables, kept chickens and a pig if possible. Women worked in the fields, also made the clothes and looked after the family. There was no mains sewerage and older inhabitants still remember the buckets being emptied at 9 pm. If the breadwinner was ill there was poverty and Mr Tom Rowley started a branch of the Manchester Unity of Oddfellows which helped, if the family could afford the contributions.

The Barley Sheaf Inn had a chequered history. Generations ago one of the Fisher rectors would call at the inn, rattling his stick across a barred window telling customers it was time for church. In 1904 the owner of Higham Hall (built 1900) found out that his footman visited the inn after church, so he bought the house and closed the business. Two semi-detached houses now stand on the site. The former blacksmith's is now named The Forge Garage.

Houghton-on-the-Hill

Houghton-on-the-Hill lies six miles east of Leicester on the main Leicester to Uppingham (A47) road and is about 525 ft above sea level. In the Domesday entry of 1086 the name is spelled 'Hohton' meaning 'spur of a hill'.

Houghton was based on six springs, the water from one was believed by the Victorians to be good for the eyes. The village pump can still be seen at the bottom of Scotland Lane, but the site of the village well is now covered by the telephone box!

The oldest surviving building is St Catharine's church. Parts of the present ironstone building date from the 13th century. The earliest surviving houses are part timber-framed. The old manor house (now called Church Farm) has a timber-framed back wing on an ironstone base with a brick front added in 1718. There are three houses dating from the 16th century, or earlier, with their original cruck trusses (two retaining thatched roofs).

After 1765 more land was turned over to pasture and by 1936 there was only nine acres being ploughed. There would have been a variety of livestock but records show that in 1896 the village sheepwasher collected 16s 8d for dipping 4,000 sheep. In 1851 nearly half the population were farmers, graziers or agricultural workers. The village was self-contained with two carpenters, wheelwrights, butchers, bakers, blacksmiths, shopkeepers, a miller, bricklayer, mole catcher, toll collector; and three framework knitters and shoemakers, and four tailors. There were also three public houses, and two carriers who would journey to and from Leicester each week to transport villagers and supplies.

The population rose to nearly 600 in 1951 but major development in the 1970s dramatically increased the population to 1,703 in 1981 (with approximately 1,900 today). Main Street is now a conservation area to try to conserve the character of the village but most of the small 'one-up, one-down' cottages have been converted into larger dwellings. Today, agriculture has gone full circle and most of the land is again ploughed, there are now only 400 sheep in the parish. Less than 2% of the population are farmers, graziers or agricultural workers and village facilities now include a playing field, village hall, and school; two garages, public houses, and general stores, and a post office.

Before the easy travelling of today most entertainment had to be generated within the village. Most festivals celebrated village and national events. In 1772 five bells were hung in the church tower and celebrated with a Feast Sunday on 29th November. This probably became an annual event as in the 1800s the Houghton Feast was always held on the first Sunday after the 29th September.

An excuse for a party was Brew Day. Mr William Ward of Manor Farm brewed beer in a large copper and Brew Day was held once a year just before haymaking. Unfortunately this custom ended in 1923.

The event of the year then became an Annual Fete held on the first Saturday in August. This became so popular that in August 1950 the Midland Red Bus Company had to provide numerous buses to transport from Leicester most of the 1,800 people who attended.

The village is still a thriving community with the village hall (built in 1921) booked every day of the week by local clubs and societies. The first Saturday in August is now a Petticoat Lane Sale raising funds for the church and village hall. Items collected from the village take a week to sort and the two day sale raised over £2,000 in 1988.

Humberstone

Humberstone is mentioned in Domesday as a small hamlet, but it has been within the city of Leicester since 1934. Locals still 'go to the village', much of which has changed. The Humberstone is a large block of granite, thought to have been a glacial erratic, and still lies in a local field. Legends and superstitions surround it. In the early 1800s the farmer who owned the field levelled off the top and filled in the ditch to facilitate ploughing, after which he never prospered and was reduced to poverty and died in the workhouse. About 100 yards to the north-east was a plot of land known as Hell Hole Furlong.

Originally there were two manors, one being a resting place for monks coming from Launde or Ingarsby to Leicester Abbey. Records show a building there in 1220. If a Brother arrived at 8 am he had breakfast and

90

beer; if at noon, dinner and beer; if at night, supper and lodging, but he had to leave before breakfast. This was known as the Martival or Haselrige manor.

The Hotoft manor was acquired by that family in the early 1300s. In the church is the tomb of Richard Hotoft, who died in 1415. The church, probably the third one on the same site, had as its first rector Richard of Gloucester, instituted in 1229. In 1617 Robert Adams, vicar, was ejected as his views were 'found to be offensive to his parishioners'. He went to Mountsorrel and there founded a school and established a vigorous group of dissenters, and got into serious trouble again.

There was a Hall at Humberstone, demolished in 1928. Its main drive, an avenue of redwood trees, still exists, as do several cottages which were on the estate, distinguishable by their red terracotta chimney pots with a 'barley sugar stick' pattern.

More and more old village features disappear, to be replaced by much that is out of character, but there are still magnificent chestnut trees and one thatched cottage.

Humberstone Garden City 🦜

Not a great many people know how 'The Anchor Tenants' of Garden City got its name. The following story will explain how this extraordinary community of people living in 143 houses on the outskirts of Leicester began.

As long ago as the early 1900s a group of far-sighted gentlemen agreed upon an idea of forming a housing company, to meet the requirements of their fellow workers in the Anchor Boot Company. Consequently 50 acres of land was acquired east of Leicester, a quarter of a mile further on through Humberstone village. Plans for this venture were laid out attractively and foundations were laid. In 1908 the first pair of houses were completed on Keyham Lane and a suitable plaque installed to commemorate the occasion. A silver trowel used at the time has recently been discovered and is now in the hands of the present Vice-Chairman.

As no shops or services were available it fell to the tenants to support themselves, therefore several businesses flourished. It was Mark Freeman who kept the chimneys swept. Harry Bowerman drove the only bus down the winding road through Humberstone to the tram terminus at the Park, refusing to take the bus out until he was satisfied that it was worth his while. Bill Duffin delivered the coal – no gas fires in those days and electricity had not reached there then.

If one needed medicines, such as castor oil, linseed oil, camphorated oil, violet powder or Fullers Earth, they were to be found at Willow-dene, Laburnum Road. If you wanted to learn to play the piano or the organ you applied to Albert Golland, Professor of Music, Fern Rise. The roads were aptly named after trees and flowers such as Chestnut Avenue, Laburnum Road, Fern Rise and Lilac Avenue. The tenants had their own bowling green and tennis courts, but their drama and musical evenings were held in Uppingham Road Assembly Rooms until the Laburnum Hall was built in 1937.

One feels sure the founders of this original community would be pleased to see that the property is well maintained and is run efficiently by today's committee.

Hungarton

Hungarton is a small conservation village seven miles east of Leicester, with 57 houses. Surrounded by open countryside, it is in the heart of 'Quorn Country' and the hunt meets regularly on Fridays during the season, often from the Black Boy Inn or one of the three country houses nearby. Its most famous member, Prince Charles, can often be seen riding through the village.

The parish of Hungarton covers a relatively large area, over 4,000 acres. In earlier times there were four distinct settlements, Hungarton, Baggrave, Quenby and Ingarsby. At the time of the Domesday Book it was Ingarsby that was mentioned as a 'larger than average settlement'. However, that settlement was cleared by Leicester Abbey in 1469. Ingarsby Hall now stands near the site, which can be seen as a series of mounds and ditches today. Quenby and Baggrave were already in decline at this time and now both sites have country houses standing on them. Hungarton evolved into the village almost as it is today. The Baggrave estate also built a small number of houses.

The church of St John the Baptist is the oldest building in the village, the main part dating from the 14th century, with some additions made in the 15th century. Standing on a small bluff, it has a magnificent view over towards Quenby Hall. The weathered appearance is due to the soft Marketing, which was quarried locally at Tilton on the Hill.

The three country houses within the parish, Baggrave Hall, Ingarsby Hall and Quenby Hall, are all imposing buildings, with Quenby and Baggrave set in large estates. Quenby Hall is cited as one of the finest examples of a Jacobean house surviving today.

In the past the village had both a cricket team and tennis team, playing other villages in the area. Both have long been disbanded, but there is an enthusiastic sports club organising a tennis tournament on the village court, which doubles as a netball court for the Boxing Day match. Every July the village is turned into a giant race track for the 'Hungarton Seven' mile road race, with 400 runners competing in one of the hilliest races in the country.

There were two inns in the village, the Ashby Arms, the name showing connections with Quenby Hall, was in existence in the 18th century, and closed sometime in the 1930s to become a working farm. The Black Boy Inn is still open today. It is rumoured to have got its name when a young black slave escaped from nearby Beeby and sought shelter there. The more probable explanation is that the Burnaby family, on whose land the inn was built, had a blackamore's head in their family crest.

There has been one Lord Hungarton in the history of the village. The former Mr Archibald Crawford of Manor Farm was raised to the peerage for his services to the country, after the Second World War when he was a member of the Agriculture Commission responsible for food.

Hungarton today is still a picturesque village and although there is no longer a central meeting place, no school or shop, there remains a strong community spirit and all local events are well supported.

Illston on the Hill

The village is a very old one. It was originally a Saxon settlement and it was mentioned in the Domesday Book.

The church was recorded in 1220 as being a chapelry of Noseley and Carlton Curlieu, being served by these churches in alternate years. The font is Saxon with a Norman base, there is Saxon work in the chancel and part of a Saxon cross in the churchyard.

The main street of Illston is part of an ancient trackway, 'twice as old as the Roman Gartree Road'. There were two inns on the route, the Sun Inn where the old Post Office is now and the Fox and Goose which is still in use. There is reputedly a poltergeist in the upper part which moves things about during the night.

Next to the Fox and Goose is a house called the 'Firs'. It was originally 'Firs Farm'. At the end of the main street is the manor house. The earliest record of a manor in Illston is 1086. The present house which was built in 1590 in ironstone, was later enlarged in brick.

The forge, situated in the main street, is over 100 years old. Henry

Payne was the first farrier and he was succeeded by his daughter, always known as 'Flo'. On her death Martin Deacon bought the property and now works there with four assistants.

In the early 1900s, continuing the agricultural tradition, there were seven farms in the village. They all had milking cows and kept a pig for bacon. Cattle were driven by road to Leicester (nine miles) setting off in the early morning at 4 am. Now this has all changed. There is only one farm left. Illston is a conservation village but in the commuter belt. The post office and shop closed ten years ago and the morning papers are delivered by the postman. As well as the working forge there is a market garden and on the outskirts of the village Padley's Poultry Farm, which employs several local people.

In the early part of this century a carrier who lived in the village would pick up goods from Leicester for a fee. 'Rosebud', the weekly bus in the 1920s, was quite famous, having been named by the owner's daughter, a Mr Charles Palmer who lived here. As well as being used as a bus 'Rosebud' served other purposes. With the top lifted off (which took four men) she carried coal from the Great Glen railway wharf. For some years the Midland Red Bus ran a twice weekly service to Leicester and once a week to Market Harborough. Today there is only a weekly bus to Leicester.

Kegworth

Kegworth lies just inside Leicestershire on the banks of the river Soar. The main A6 road runs through the centre of the village, and to the west is the M1 motorway. Sometimes it feels as though the village is in the middle of an island, with heavy lorries passing the Market Place all day long. Also close by is the East Midlands airport, with parts of the village lying directly under the flight path – in fact in 1989 there was a very near miss when a British Midland Airways aircraft narrowly avoided crashing onto the village, instead hitting the M1 motorway, with the sad loss of 47 lives.

The parish church of St Andrew stands overlooking the Market Place. The present building is one of the largest parish churches in Leicestershire. There has been a church on this site for a thousand years. The piece of ground overlooking Nottingham Road was covered in bushes up to the 1920s and was called the Cunnery. When a new water drain was laid, the path up to the vestry door was one mass of skeletons – as if there had been a battle and the bodies had been thrown in anyhow. Before the ground was filled in all the bones had to be re-interred.

At the bottom of Mill Lane there used to be a plaster mill with a large waterwheel. There was a waterway called the Mill Dam. In later years the site became a basketwork makers and the village women used to peel the osiers in a hot water tank roughly 12 ft by 4 ft. The women stood on either side of the tank, stripping the osiers with their hands stained bright red. The osiers were willows grown at the nearby Ratcliffe and Kegworth sewage farm.

Farming played a large part in Kegworth life. In the 18th century stockinger's shops were much in evidence. Michael Harrison had a stockinger's shop at the back of Harrison House (one of the oldest houses at present – 1575). He often worked all night to get his orders ready and this job was done by the light of a paraffin lamp.

In the summer of 1812 Kegworth's most famous character took up residence at a house known as 'The Cedars' on London Road. Thomas Moore, the Irish poet, requested Lord Moira to help him 'find out a house, that will do for the residence of a poet'. Before taking possession of the house, Moore requested that someone be installed in the house to take care of it – and to eject 'the gentleman upstairs', referring to the phantom of a former tenant, thought to be a butler who had been murdered in the house.

One of the most important houses in the village is the Great House, which was built in 1698 in the reign of William and Mary, its architecture influenced by the Dutch. It is said that ghosts have been seen in this house, particularly a large elderly lady dressed in grey tweeds.

The school used to be in The Dragwell, the school governess being Miss Unwin, who had a reputation for caning for the most trivial reasons, such as holes in shoes or marks on sailor collars. Children were too frightened to go to school and too frightened to stay away!

On Shrove Tuesday the 'Pancake Bell' was rung at 11 am which was a sign for going home, the rest of the day being holiday. Then games of battledore and shuttlecock, or whip and top would be played.

In the summer evenings games were arranged on the main road. Races were held from the old Three Cranes public house (which was kept by Mr and Mrs Beale, who had 13 children) down to the Britannia Inn. There was not much traffic then, only the beer drays bringing home the empties to Wells Brewery on the Market Place.

Every summer a carnival is held on the Hallstone Meadows – a tradition which goes back to the Wakes Fair Weekend and the Hospital Association Carnival which was established in 1923. Britain's longest running Steam and Traction Engine Rally is held at the same time.

Ketton 🦋

The river Chater, which gave the village its name, flows quietly through the fields of Ketton, past the old water mill, under the ancient bridge by the 13th century church of St Mary and on through the meadows to join the river Welland running eastward to Stamford.

Ketton's long village street displays a pleasing assortment of old houses and cottages, many built in the 18th and 19th centuries of local limestone. Some of the larger houses were built in the oolitic limestone for which Ketton's quarries have been famous for centuries. This excellent stone was used in the Tower of London, Lambeth Palace and many of the buildings in Cambridge.

There are reminders of the past in the names of some of Ketton's lanes and houses. At one corner of Bull Lane, now the site of the filling station, stood the Pied Bull public house, destroyed by fire in 1935. On the opposite corner, The Old Aveland Arms, now a private house, was one of eleven public houses in the village. Now only the Northwick Arms and the Railway Inn remain. There were three quoits beds in Ketton, the one opposite the post office giving Quoits Cottage in Bull Lane its name. This popular inter-village game was played until the 1920s and Mr A. Knox of Ketton was all-England champion three times. Redmile's Lane, leading to a house which was once the workhouse, took its name from a Farmer Redmile. A former resident of St Mary's House in the High Street gave his name to Hunts Lane.

During the first half of this century St Mary's House was a reform home for girls. They attended chapel daily in the adjacent Bishop Clayton Hall and were cared for by nuns. An underground passage from the house led to the laundry, where the girls worked. This building is now the bungalows 82 and 84 High Street.

In the early part of the century there were three butchers, three bakers and tradesmen of all sorts so the village was self-sufficient. Many housewives took their Sunday joints and Yorkshire pudding to be cooked at the bakehouse for a few pence.

There have been no stocks at Stocks Hill since 1890, nor is there a hill and the 1887 Jubilee Monument is now known as The Fountain, although there is no water where once a stand-pipe provided a supply for the village.

The railway station which was used by schoolchildren, shoppers and workers closed in 1966 but the Victorian signal box is still manned.

On the site of the old school near Stocks Hill is a branch library: an amenity much appreciated and well used. A new primary school was built on an adjacent field and opened in 1971.

Many Ketton people are self-employed in farming and various other occupations, some commute to the towns and cities and others form part of the 450 strong work force at the Castle Cement Works, whose huge buildings dominate the eastern approach to the village.

Keyham 🦔

Keyham, in the past variously spelled Keam, Keame and Cayham, is a small village of some 55 houses, lying approximately six miles east of Leicester.

All Saints' church was probably built during the 15th century and is largely of ironstone. Plaques and headstones commemorate the Wood-cock, Woodford, Clayton and Miles families, all long associated with Keyham, and in the church tower it is recorded that Thomas Woodcock in his will of 1680 made provision for '20 hundredweight of good pit coals' to be given to 'four of the poorest widows' and 'also 30 two penny loaves to be distributed among the poorest inhabitants' on the feast day of St Thomas the Apostle. This custom has long since been discontinued but many years later five charity cottages were built in the village, of which four are still in use. The fifth was sold and the revenue raised by the sale was used to improve the basic amenities of the remaining cottages.

There is no school in the village as the Board School, built in 1885, was closed and sold in September 1948. The building was converted to a private dwelling in 1966. Prior to the establishment of this school there had been a 'boys school' which two of the oldest inhabitants of the village still recall hearing about. This 'school' consisted of a small square covered area opposite the village pub where the local lads would have received a rather rudimentary education for a few years.

Before the village hall was built in the late 1920s dances and meetings were held in the school. During the early part of this century there was a flourishing cricket club, matches being played on one of the fields belonging to Pear Tree Farm.

Like the school, the village shop-cum-post office was converted to a private house after its owner, Miss Gertie Healey retired in 1978. She was awarded the BEM for 40 years service in the post office but in fact her connection with the shop was for far longer than that. Her mother had originally started the shop in the early 1900s, which she later took over. The smithy which was next to the shop and also in use in the early part of this century was later converted into a garage for the house.

Over the past 60 to 70 years the character of the village has altered radically. One could not now conceive of anyone starting up a foundry in the village, yet in 1911 Mr Robert Harrison did just that. It flourished and provided valuable employment for a number of men in the village. In addition, at a time when there were few cars or buses, it provided a valuable means of communication with Leicester. Many a Keyham woman came to rely on regular trips into Leicester with the foundry van and the Healeys also relied on it for stocking their shop. Times changed, however, and in 1939 the foundry closed in Keyham and transferred to Leicester.

Although the village is surrounded by open fields there is only one working farm in the village, on the parish boundary. The roads are tarred and the cows no longer come through the village twice daily for milking.

Kibworth Beauchamp

Kibworth Beauchamp is situated to the south of the A6 road, six miles north-west of Market Harborough and nine miles south of Leicester. It is adjacent to its smaller twin, Kibworth Harcourt, which lies mainly to the north. At the time of the Domesday Book, Kibworth Beauchamp recorded 28 inhabitants but by 1223 was sufficiently thriving to be granted the right to hold a weekly market. This, however, was short-lived and Kibworth was destined to remain a village rather than grow into a market town.

Its present population is around 4,500, three times that recorded in the 1881 census. As with many other Leicestershire village communities, hosiery has played an important role in its history. Some three-storey homes on Weir Road are still known as 'the factory houses', a throwback to days when framework knitting machines were housed and used there. The last surviving hosiery factory, Johnson & Barnes, closed in 1970. Many of the older village people used to work there. The connection still exists though, as many senior and middle management people from the Leicester knitwear trade live in the village.

There is a long tradition of good education in the village. According to local tradition, the Kibworth Beauchamp grammar school was founded in 1471 – though its first proven mention is in 1559. Children from all over South Leicestershire travelled to the school until in 1964 it moved to Oadby, where the Kibworth connection was maintained in the name of the new Oadby Beauchamp school. The old grammar school buildings, including the fine 1725 headmaster's house, are now used by Kibworth High School.

A short distance up the High Street stands Beauchamp manor house. Somewhere around 1250 this came into the hands of the Beauchamp family who became Earls of Warwick, and from whom the village got the second part of its name. The manor is a real gem of old architecture, in the 'H' style and is enhanced with beautiful gardens at the rear. The clock tower on the corner of the stable block is quite a prominent feature and as it is always kept to the correct time must have enabled many villagers to catch buses and to get to work on time.

Above the railway, watching over the whole village, stands the parish church of St Wilfrid, dating mainly from the 14th century though its medieval spire collapsed in 1825 and the present tower was built shortly afterwards.

The Co-op store in the High Street has recently been extended and made into a modern supermarket. Various other shops are on either side of the street including the busy post office and Country Fare where a welcome cup of coffee may be obtained. The farmhouse next to the Co-op helps to retain some of the rural village character. Two very attractive Georgian houses stand opposite to the Co-op and an interesting feature just by them is an old mud wall, the only remaining evidence of a rare type of cottage.

The cricket field is up beyond the houses on the left of Fleckney Road. This gets quite a lot of support and on several occasions the windows of the houses opposite have been broken by some of the team's tremendous sixes! Further on, and round to the right, Warwick Road presents a very pleasant country walk, eventually joining the Wistow Road and to the Grand Union canal. Here one can pass some tranquil hours just watching the boats proceeding through the locks or just enjoying the countryside. In the spring, cowslips and ladysmocks may be found in the field by the water and the hedges are splattered with snowy May blossom – it is a beautiful, peaceful place to be.

Kibworth Harcourt 🌿

People have lived in Kibworth Harcourt for a very long time. The Romans were certainly here, as many finds of jewellery, pottery and weapons testify, and a farming community seems to have evolved dominated by larger villa estates. The large mound in the centre of the village, known locally as 'The Munt' is now thought to mark the grave of a wealthy farmer of this era.

After the Norman Conquest the lands around Kibworth were given to the De Harcourts, thus adding 'Harcourt' to Kibworth. The Kibworth lands eventually came into the possession of Merton College, Oxford, which still remains a major landowner in the district and has had the effect of restricting excessive expansion of the village into surrounding farmland, thus retaining much of its original character.

In Main Street (formerly known as the Kings Highway or Church Street) is the Three Horseshoes inn, part of which was once a blacksmith's, and the manor house, behind which are two medieval fish ponds. The old market place at one time had a village cross and pump. The cross has long since gone but the pump was recently restored by the Conservation Society. 'The Old House', standing opposite, was the first brick-built building in the village, dating from 1678.

Albert Street was formerly known as 'Hog Lane' from the fact that a pig market was once held there. At the end of this street is a group of 18th and 19th century cottages known as 'The City', though the origin of the name is obscure. On the nearby hilltop is the windmill, dating back to 1711. The last load of corn was ground there around 1925 and Charlie Smith, the last miller, lived in a cottage above the Three Horseshoes until his death. The windmill, one of the few post mills remaining in the country, has been restored.

The Rose and Crown inn was once a busy posting house where most of the coaches which passed through Kibworth (up to 24 by day and night) used to change horses. There is a tombstone in the churchyard which commemorates the death of one coachman who was killed when his vehicle overturned.

The church of St Wilfrid, although in Beauchamp, is shared by both parishes. Older residents recall that the north door of the church was always known as the 'Harcourt Door', and brides from Harcourt always entered and left by this door.

Parts of Kibworth Harcourt were declared a conservation area in 1983 and the Conservation Society has planted many bulbs, shrubs and trees to enhance the appearance of the area.

Kilby 🌿

Kilby is a small village of some 80 households situated in a valley off the A50, often referred to as 'The Turnpike', about seven miles south of Leicester.

In the 19th century much of the village was part of the Wistow estate although there were some private landowners. Many of the people worked on the land or were in domestic service, but almost as many worked in the knitting industry, some on their own frames at home, but many travelling to factories in Fleckney and Wigston.

The oldest buildings in the village are 17th century. Part of the Dog and Gun, which is still thriving and The Black Swan, which has been turned into a private house, date back to this time. There are no important houses here. In 1980 Blaby Council listed a number of buildings such as The Old Bakery and Manor Farm to prevent demolition and development.

A building situated behind the churchyard is believed to be of considerable historical interest. The old village, as recorded in the Domesday Book, was round the church which now stands isolated some quarter of a mile from the village. The present church of St Mary Magdalen was built in 1857.

The greatest change in the village took place after the First World War, when Lord Cottesloe of Wistow Hall sold it to Leicestershire County Council, to provide 50 acre smallholdings for ex-service men. There were 16 of these and life at that time was still fairly primitive. Each farmer had about ten cows, which he milked twice daily, and to eke out a meagre living he also kept a flock of sheep, a few cattle, hens and two pigs, to keep the family in bacon and ham. He grew corn to sell and mangolds to feed the animals in the winter. All cultivation was done by horse power.

Until the Second World War Kilby was self-sufficient, having its own butcher, baker, carpenter, blacksmith, post office, shop and two public houses. There was also regular transport to Wigston and Leicester.

Kilby is now a prosperous village. The ex-service generation have all now died – some of them remaining in Kilby until the end of their lives. Several of the farmhouses were sold but the land, still owned by the County Council, has been divided amongst the new generation of farmers who each have up to 100 cows and all kinds of expensive machinery available to the modern farming business.

Although these working farms give it an agricultural feel, the majority of the community consists of a complete cross-section of retired people, businessmen, teachers and employees in all trades and professions, who commute to the surrounding areas.

Kimcote & Walton 🦚

The villages of Kimcote and Walton combine to form one parish. The church being situated in Kimcote reduces the importance of Walton to an associate hamlet.

Many stockingers worked in this parish during the 19th century, their buildings now demolished. In the earlier part of this century, successful businesses were conducted in Walton by carpenters and wheelwrights, decorators, bakers, blacksmiths, bricklayers and bootmakers. All now have disappeared; a general store with post office and one public house now remain. Apart from a modern mushroom farm at Kimcote, today's employment is found outside the parish.

The farming fraternity manage their holdings with labour from within their own households, some seeking help from contractors to accomplish the urgent seasonal tasks. Individual cowmen, shepherds and waggoners are now only a memory, their traditions overtaken by technology.

Walton once had a church, dedicated to St James. The site is no longer known but it seems to have become defunct about 1630. An old legend has it that an attempt was made to build a church at Walton, but as fast as it was built during the day, the Devil destroyed it at night. This may have been an attempt to replace the lost church in face of strong opposition.

Another old legend concerns the death of a pauper in a house through which ran the boundary dividing Kimcote from Knaptoft. The body lay across this boundary and the problem was which parish was responsible for its burial. The solution – the parish which contained his feet!

Two annual events used to be celebrated in the village. First, Plough Monday, when groups of youths, heavily disguised, visited homes likely to give monetary rewards, singing 'Put your hand in your purse' etc. In times past it was the practice to plough up the causeway in front of premises where favourable response did not materialise, hence the heavy disguise.

The second event was May Day, when a May Queen was elected and paraded around the parish with attendants, bedecked with flowers, singing such songs as 'Here we come a Maying' etc.

Walton Feast Week following the 6th of August proved an attraction to the surrounding district with a visit from a fairground company. There were club dinners, with dancing in the streets and general high jinks, but all was halted by the First World War, the fairground company being disbanded.

Previous generations would talk about an ancient market here, quoting such landmarks as 'Hog Lane', the 'Hen Pleck' and 'Cattle Bank' as proof. It is assumed it could have been associated with the Feast Week. These names are still known but without identification.

'The Old Hall' at Walton which must, in its heyday, have housed the more influential families, was of close timbered wattle and daub medieval construction, built on the three bay system. The scribed carpenters' marks can still be seen. The roadway Hall Lane and Hall Close opposite, must have taken its name.

Kirby Bellars

Kirby Bellars is a small select village, though widely spread, with farms up to 1½ miles away.

Kirby Hall was once the home of Colonel and Mrs Muir. They held an annual garden fete on their lawns and everyone felt rather grand parading up and down in fancy dress while Mrs Muir judged the costumes. They had a butler, Mr Annerley, and Tommy Warren 'The Boot', also a chauffeur Mr Dawes, who were housed in nearby cottages. Cottage No 1 (once the 'Flying Childers') is now called 'Lazy Acre', the home of David Weston the artist who is famous for his magnificent paintings of steam trains.

Ted Hazelwood lived at 'Abrahams Orchard' and was leader of the handbell team. After his death the bells were put in 'moth balls'. Today they are once again much in use – Mrs Sampey gives lessons to youngsters and adults in the village, and the bells are enjoyed at local concerts and church services – particularly at Christmas time.

The chapel (now Druids Lodge) had a thriving Sunday school. The highlight of the year was the Anniversary. The visitors would go to tea in various homes, when the best tea-cloths and china appeared and no expense was spared. Sunday school was at 2 pm, followed by Church Service at 3 pm, so you had to get a move on if you were in the choir, and chapel again at 6 pm; not much spare time was left on Sundays!

Washdyke Lane was named after 'the washing of the sheep'. It was compulsory for farmers to take their sheep annually to the river to be washed. The sheep were pushed in and two men holding poles with long hooks attached, pulled them out on to dry land. They would then be taken home – a day's task. In the summer, when the water-tubs became empty, washing water had to be fetched from the river in a dolly-tub balanced on a barrow. The water was heated in an outside copper, then the family would have a bath – the cleanest first!

St Peter's church is of 13th and 14th century origin. Much construction took place in the early 1200s. In 1319 the church was enlarged by the addition of the south and north aisles. The south aisle contains two alabaster figures dating from 1360–1370, supposedly of the murdered Roger de Beler and his mother Alice.

Large modern houses have appeared in the village and many older properties have been restored but Kirby is still a quiet village. If you are looking for a beautiful place – visit the churchyard, or walk by the river in the cricket field, where peace and tranquillity can be found.

Kirby Muxloe 🦚

There has been a settlement here since prehistoric times and there are indications of a Roman road, but the name of the village was derived from a 9th century Danish settler called 'Carbi'. Some 500 years later when it was known as 'Kirby', the name 'Muckles' was added to distinguish the village from the nearby Kirkby Mallory. The name Kirby Muxloe was established in the mid-18th century.

In the Domesday Book (1086) it was recorded as a farming village with less than 50 inhabitants. The population gradually increased through the ages, the Industrial Revolution bringing work other than agriculture to the community and the current population is about 5,000. It is mainly a residential area with easy access into Leicester, and by means of trunk roads and motorways, to many other places of employment.

The village has an unusual 15th century red brick castle, although it is a castle in name only. Lord Hastings commenced building a fortified house in 1480 but it was incomplete at the time of his execution three years later and so it has remained.

St Bartholomew's, dating back to the 14th century, stands on the site of an earlier church recorded in 1168 and was restored in 1858. A church hall was built in 1924 and when Kirby Muxloe became a parish in 1930, St Bartholomew's was established as the parish church.

During the 18th century various attempts were made to establish nonconformist religious meeting places and eventually, in 1897 a chapel was built at the western end of Main Street. The chapel was demolished when the village was bombed on 19th November 1940 and the present Free church, built on the same site, was opened on 12th September 1953.

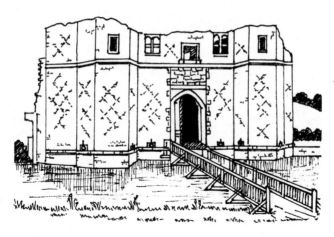

Kirby Muxloe Castle

The village suffered severe bomb damage one night during the Second World War, when enemy aircraft being pursued after a raid on Coventry dropped their remaining bombs as they fled. In addition to the chapel, a house on Station Road was destroyed and some 350 houses were badly damaged making 400 homeless. Nearly every house suffered some damage and the west window of St Bartholomew's church was blown out. Fortunately no-one was killed although several people were injured.

Early in the 19th century attempts were made to establish a day school in the village and in 1854 Kirby Muxloe Church school was opened. On the corner of Main Street and Ratby Lane a lovely old 'Swiss' style house was built in 1858 for use as a school and it served this purpose until the Council primary school in Barwell Road opened in 1910. Subsequently the old house became a Sunday school and later a vicarage. It is now a family home called 'Parson's Farewell' and is in part a craft and tea shop.

No village is complete without an alehouse and the original Royal Oak was first licensed in 1810. The existing Royal Oak on Main Street was built on the same site in 1970.

Kirkby Mallory 🌿

Nine miles to the west of Leicester lies the village of Kirkby Mallory, standing 400 feet above sea-level, and home to 300 inhabitants.

Pleasant farmland surrounds the village, which was known as Cherchebei in the Domesday Book. In the reign of Henry II, the manor was vested in the Mallory family. Down through the years ownership passed from the Noel family to the eldest son of Sir Clobery Noel, who became Viscount Wentworth in 1762.

Kirkby Mallory has historical connections with Lord Byron, who married Baroness Wentworth. Their daughter Ada Augusta married the first Earl of Lovelace, and was a brilliant mathematician, assisting Charles Babbage in evolving a system which was the forerunner of today's computers.

Quite a number of villagers were employed in work at the Hall and its estate, as gardeners, grooms and general servants. Farming and nearby coal mines provided work too.

All Saints' church contains many plaques to the memory of some of the noble families who lived at the Hall, also past villagers. Social events centred around the church, rectory and school, such as garden fetes, whist drives and dances.

A forge behind one of the old cottages was used by the blacksmith as lots of horses worked on the farms. People owned large gardens and cultivated allotments too, so were quite self-sufficient. A cricket team was formed around 1920, and still carries on, using one of the farmer's fields in the centre of the village. This makes for a typically English scene on a pleasant summer's day!

Although the school, dated 1865, was closed by the Education authorities some years ago, it is still in use as a village hall.

Unfortunately, the fine mansion, known as Kirkby Hall, is no longer in existence, but the extensive parkland which surrounded it is now the site of Mallory Park, the motor racing circuit. This was started in 1955 by a local businessman. The old coach houses and stable buildings are now converted to a restaurant and hotel connected with the circuit.

Knossington 🌿

A pleasant village in High Leicestershire bordering Rutland, well endowed with mature trees planted a century ago, Knossington is 600 feet above sea level. The river Gwash rises here then flows into the Welland.

The remains of a Saxon warrior were found on Sconsborough Hill, and were reinterred in 'Whalebones' orchard. The Whalebones had a whale's jaw bone arching over the gate.

Three roads radiate from the village centre, leaving a large open space which accommodates the village pump; in the 18th century there was also a permanent maypole. In recent years various forms of May Day celebrations have been revived. The village hall, formerly the old school, faces the centre and provides recreational facilities.

A new school was built and given to the village in 1901 by Mr A. L. Duncan who came to live at the newly built Grange in 1867. He also built stables, houses for estate workers, the forge and restored the church.

The population rose from 126 in 1801 to 319 in 1871. It is now about 250. For years the village was an independent community, having a corn grinding mill, baker, butcher, blacksmith, shoemaker, builders, dressmaker, tailor, apiarist, carpenter/painter/decorator/undertaker, wheelwright and a weekly carrier. The doctor and nurse came from Somerby by horse or cycle.

The stone built church of St Peter dates from the 13th century with a square tower. Near the church is one of the oldest houses – the Manor House, 16th–17th century. The original manor house (now farm) is in Owston Road. There is only one public house now – the other closed in 1930.

Mrs Straker at the Grange died in 1948. The estate was sold. Her workers retired or found new jobs and the village was no longer a self-contained community. The Grange became a choir and prep school for some years; now it is a private remedial school for boys, giving employment to many villagers. With the sale of the Grange a lot of the mature timber was felled including the two coverts, some of which are being replanted.

Fourteen council houses were built in 1948 and these brought in new people; eight houses were allocated for agricultural workers. There was an upsurge in the village school life. The village hall was redecorated and refurbished to provide extra space for the village school, and returning social activities. Now the village has lost all its tradesmen, two shops and post office. The population has altered and farms are fully mechanised. Knossington is now a conservation village.

Langham 🐚

It would be scarcely an exaggeration to say that Langham (population 1,200) is a village that has almost everything: a beautiful 13th century church and a mid-Victorian Baptist chapel, a modern school and a late-Victorian village hall, all well-used, maintained and cared for. This is a living village, neither a dormitory suburb nor an ancient monument.

Four village shops, one of which incorporates the post office, provide the necessities of life. All four shops are owned by either 'native' Langham families or they have close Langham connections. Three public houses, each with its own style and 'regulars', provide good food and drink.

The most notable building is the mainly Gothic parish church dedicated to St Peter and St Paul. It is unusually large for a village church, light and lofty. It has a square tower with a clock on one face and decorated spire topped by a newly re-gilded weather cock; a useful landmark for travellers.

The church has a fine peal of bells – the Captain of the Bells is Fred Hubbard, member of one of Langham's oldest families. One ancestor's name is carved on a roof beam with the date 1783, following restoration work when he was churchwarden.

Langham's most illustrious son was Simon de Langham, born in 1310. He became both the Chancellor of England, and the Archbishop of Canterbury, and finally a Cardinal. He died in Avignon in 1376. He was given a splendid tomb in Westminster Abbey, the nave of which was rebuilt by the money he had left.

Langham has Rutland's only brewery, Ruddles, whose fame has spread far beyond county boundaries. It is the village's largest single employer with a workforce of over a hundred.

Agriculture is still important to Langham as it has been since Anglo-Saxon times when this 'long village' acquired its name. A dozen families farm or provide the necessary attendant services; from smallholdings to farms of many acres. Sadly the small milking herd belonging to Langham Dairies had to be dispersed because of strict EEC regulations.

Allotments, first established 1835, continue to flourish though they no longer grow corn: the original crop. In 1889 Mr Nourish set up his threshing machine just off Melton Road, and threshed the allotment corn for 6d a bag. His grandson Dick Nourish of Hayes Farm carries on the tradition, still specialising in agricultural machinery.

Horses have, for centuries, been part of Langham life. The Cottesmore

Hunt Kennels are less than a mile away and the hunt meets in the village every season. Langham House, now a private nursing home, was once a hunting box.

The brook meanders through the village and the sheepwash on Ashwell Road, once used regularly by village flocks, is now remembered by a new house of that name.

Forge Cottage on Well Street, its walls covered with horseshoes, shows where the smithy stood for 150 years. Its present occupant Ben Walker remembers the last blacksmith working there.

Victorian cottages, their dark red bricks made in the brickyard up by Langham pastures over 150 years ago, are interspersed with modern houses. Picturesque thatched cottages and graceful old houses of local stone all combine to form this most interesting and delightful picture of Langham, the village with nearly everything.

The Langtons

There are five Langtons near Market Harborough; Church, Thorpe, East, West and Tur Langton.

Church Langton was known as 'Langtone' – 'long settlement' – in the Domesday Book. It is on a ridge and the mother church, St Peter's, is a notable landmark. In 1503, when England was a Catholic country, the Pope sent an Italian named Polydore Vergil to the living. He stayed in England for 28 years and wrote a history of England at the invitation of Henry VII.

The most famous rector of all was William Hanbury. He established extensive plantations and gardens in Tur Langton and Gumley, getting seeds even from North America. From the sale of seeds and plants, he wanted to establish a fund for the upkeep of the Langtons' churches, to fund a hospital, a school, a great minster and library. He organised three music festivals between 1759 and 1761. Handel's *Messiah* was performed for the first time in an English church at Church Langton and drew fashionable society from far and near. Most of Hanbury's plans came to nothing, but he founded a charity which has greatly benefited the Langtons.

Many Thorpe Langton residents have fine views of the hills of the Langton Candles and the Fernie hunting country. St Leonard's is old, with a 13th century tower and spire. There is a story that, in 1782, a bellringer left the tenor bell upside down, hoping it might overturn in the

St Peter's church, The Langtons

night and wake the village. Unfortunately, it overturned next day, killing a carpenter.

The village of East Langton has pleasant little lanes. On one of them is The Grange, largely rebuilt in Georgian style by Lt Col J. D. Hignett, a great benefactor of the villages and patron of local causes. His predecessor, J. W. Logan, was Harborough's MP and supervised the building of the LNWR lines from Newark to Leicester, Hallaton and Harborough. He built a riding school and stables and the village hall, first used as a private theatre for his daughters. East Langton's fine cricket field was begun by him. In the centre of the village is The Bell Inn, the older part of which dates from the late 17th century.

West Langton, on the road to Kibworth, had most of its fields enclosed in the 16th and 17th centuries before the general enclosure of the Langtons in 1792. The Hall was built in 1631 but had late additions and alterations.

The most famous of Langton Hall's owners was Hugo Meynell, 'the father of modern fox-hunting' and founder of the Quorn Hunt. He lived in Quorn and built kennels there. He hunted over a large area stretching from Nottingham to Harborough. Because of the size of the country, he had Langton Hall as a hunting box. He was said to be 'like a regular little apple-dumpling on horse-back'.

110

Tur Langton was a Saxon village called 'Terlintone' in 1086. It has the only shop and post office in the Langtons, a village hall and two public houses. Once there were three; the third being The Chequers. Maybe it needed three inns – not because of the drunkenness of its inhabitants but because of the numbers of drovers who passed through.

Joseph Goddard, designer of Leicester's Clock Tower, was the architect for Tur Langton's red brick church, St Andrew's, begun in 1865. It is said to be 'the most striking example of High Victorian church building in Leicestershire'. All that remains of the medieval church is one arch, the north doorway, railed off next to the manor-house.

Gone are the village baker, policeman, roadman, undertaker and wheelwright of Tur Langton, the butcher and blacksmith of East Langton. Villagers include many people working in the professions and industry who commute to work.

Leire

Leire nestles near a tributary of the river Soar towards the southernmost point of the county. It is commonly thought that the settlement was so named after the ancient name of the river Soar, which was Leir, Leyre and Legre at respective times.

On this stretch of the river the village boasts two water mills, the one at the northern end, now known as Stemborough Mill, while on the southern boundary stands Leire Mill. Wheat was ground at Stemborough Mill until 1946. The present owner has restored the water wheel to its full glory.

Today the village possesses one village shop with post office, a garage and two public houses, namely the Queens Arms and The White Horse. In the 19th century the village appears to have been served by a butcher, baker, grocer, greengrocer, haberdasher, cobbler, bootmaker, wheelwright, blacksmith, village carrier and three public houses (the additional hostelry being The Bulls Head).

The oldest remaining house, now known as The Manor House and previously known as 'The Old Home' is timber framed and thatched and was built in the 17th century. Another old property, Glebe House, was built in 1793 and in the mid-19th century was used for the production of Stilton cheese.

The church of St Peter stands proud on high ground. The first recorded rector in 1210 was William de Leyre. Major alterations to the church were carried out between 1866 and 1868.

In the records of the churchwarden's accounts for the years 1718–19 is an entry 'Paid to John Bradford for one hedgehog, 2d', presumably for the purpose of killing insects in the church. Another interesting entry, 'Given to John Pinner too quarts of ale to clime in at the bell window when the key was lost, 3d'.

At the rear of Airedale Farm there is evidence of a shallow moat. Archaeological excavations have taken place in the field in the hope of establishing the existence of an old manor but nothing conclusive was established. Roman pottery and medieval paving were discovered during ground excavation for the bungalow immediately below the church.

Framework knitting was one of the main occupations in the 19th century. Many houses in the village housed framework knitting machines. Knitting is known to have taken place in three particular cottages, now known as Fern Cottage and cottages in Back Lane, which were demolished some years ago. As many dwellings were too small to house a framework knitting machine, the first 'factory' was started in buildings at Eaglesfield House.

At one time 13 charities were in existence providing blankets, bread, coal and money for the industrious poor of the village. The 'Bell Rope Piece' charity was instigated when a villager was lost on his way home in the dark via the footpath from Broughton Astley. The sound of the church bell had guided him home and in gratitude he gave the rent of a strip of meadow valued at 3s 4d per annum towards new bell ropes and for the bell to be tolled at 8 pm.

A village personality caused a problem on her departure. Jane Ladkin, landlady of The Queens Arms in the 1880s was a very big woman. When she died, her coffin was too large to go through the door and a hole had to be made in the wall! Her orchard was full of violet plum trees and she used to take a load weekly by cart to Leicester market during the season. Following this lady's death, the plum trees died.

Following the closure of the railway, the village made a valuable gain by way of a stretch of the railway cutting. A lease was negotiated with the owners for the use of this area as a nature walk and it was subsequently named Jubilee Walk. This has now been safeguarded for the future use of the village with the purchase outright by two generous parishioners. With the playing field alongside, these facilities are much enjoyed by villagers and visitors alike.

Lockington 🌿

Between the Norman Conquest and the Dissolution of the Monasteries in 1539, the land and village belonged to the Abbot of Leicester. Thus Lockington, Hemington, Castle Donington and Diseworth answered collectively as one village in the hundred of Gascote.

From 1597 to 1870 Lockington belonged to the Bainbrigge family and (from 1797) to their cousins the Storys, who sold it to Mr Nathaniel Curzon of Breedon-on-the-Hill. The estate now belongs to his great-great nephew Charles Coaker.

The church of St Nicholas is both beautiful and interesting in that it boasts an example of most periods of architecture from Norman to the present day. The northern door and font are Norman.

From 1877 to 1878 the parson was Robert Story. He is said to have shot the last brace of grouse in Charnwood Forest. Gambling and cock-fighting were added to his clerical duties and he is reputed to have held a cock fight againt the notorious Marquess of Hastings in the family pew at Lockington. His dog accompanied him to church and when one day a strange dog wandered in a fight started. The congregation tried to part them but the Rev Bob shouted from the top of the three-decker pulpit, 'Leave them alone you fools! I'll lay 10–1 on mine.'

Ted Joyce was the sexton, whose family had lived in Lockington for 400 years. He kept the Elizabethan church plate under his bed for safety (it is now in Leicester Museum). Until the outbreak of war in 1939 he rang the curfew every night at 8 pm.

'Put up your pipes and go to Lockington Wake.' A saying thought to have referred to wandering minstrels. They were reckoned a noisy nuisance and as Lockington lies at the north-western extremity of Leicestershire this seemed the furthest place to which to banish them.

Up until the 1960s the inhabitants had for centuries consisted of farmers, farm and estate workers and craftsmen and numbered between 80–100. Since then the Hall has been let as offices, the kitchen garden is now a garden centre. Cottages have been sold and new houses built. The result is that only a tiny minority of the inhabitants now rely on the village for their livelihood.

Long Clawson

The village of Long Clawson nestles under the hills at the western end of the Vale of Belvoir, about six miles from Melton Mowbray and 13 miles from Nottingham. It is first recorded in the Domesday Book as 'Clachestone', and in legal documents over the centuries is referred to as Claxton alias Long Clawson. It is actually listed twice in Domesday, probably due to an error on the part of the scribe and one wonders whether the unfortunate inhabitants found themselves suffering from two lots of taxation.

Nevertheless, there were two separate manors in Clachestone and this has lead to a belief that there were once two distinct settlements. Although there is no supporting evidence, it would go some way towards explaining the most obvious feature of the village, that Long Clawson is most certainly long! A journey from West End to East End would cover a distance of one and a quarter miles and involves negotiating 14 right-angled bends.

Long Clawson was, and essentially still is, an agricultural village. The antiquarian Leland remarked in the 16th century that here was 'good corne ground', but with the decline of arable farming in the last quarter of the 19th century most of the smallholdings were given over to pasture, a pattern that has only recently begun to change. There were once 14 farms spaced out along the length of the village with their fields stretching up into the hills and down to the river Smite.

The village was practically self-sufficient until the Second World War with a timberyard and wheelwrights, joiners, carpenters, plumbers and glaziers, blacksmiths, a saddler, shoemakers, tailors and weavers. In the 1920s it even had its own bus company. Of course, all this has changed, although the corn mill, less its sails, still stands sentinel over the village. This is not to say that there is a lack of services as there are two stores and two butchers, a bakery, two pubs, a surgery and a thriving primary school.

The changes have also had their effect on the buildings of the village and no longer can there be found any examples of the once common cob and thatch. The impressive ironstone church with its cruciform shape and crossing tower, dating from the early 14th century, still overlooks the 17th century Old Manor House and the fishermen at the pond. The church is dedicated to St Remigius. Immediately adjoining is the Castle Field which contains traces of ancient dwellings and a moat, which seems to disappear under the churchyard, thereby demonstrating its great antiquity.

Whilst Long Clawson can boast of no famous inhabitants nor was it ever the site of a battle or any other historic event, its name is known throughout the world. As long ago as 1900, Rider Haggard visited the village to learn about cheesemaking and just before the First World War farmers and smallholders combined together to form a co-operative. Nowadays, Stilton cheese from Long Clawson Dairy Ltd is sold in better class establishments all over England and in many other countries.

Long Clawson and its neighbouring village, Hose, have combined to contribute at least one often quoted saying – 'There are more whores in Hose than honest women in Long Clawson.' It is amusing to read the explanations of authors who have forgotten that at one time, the wearing of stockings was not considered respectable and therefore miss the point of the pun. Needless to say the reputation of the ladies of both villages has always been above reproach!

Loseby

A small village with an ancient church and imposing Hall. Situated in the east of the county.

In the Domesday Book of 1086 the name of the village was spelt 'Glowesbi'. Various spellings have been used down the centuries.

The Burdet family were the first known residents of Lowesby Hall. Some of the Burdets lived at Newton Burdet, now known as Cold Newton, in the parish of Loseby.

In 1615 the Hall and estate were sold for £12,040. In 1938 the 5th Marquis of Waterford, for a 100 guineas wager, jumped a five barred gate in the dining room, on his hunter *Don Juan*. He is reputed to have shot out the eyes on the Fowkes portraits, because he said they were staring at him!

The village was re-sited after the plague in the 14th century and the old village outline can be seen clearly from the air.

Lyddington

Lyddington is situated on the north-west slopes of the Welland valley. It is a mile long, most of the houses being on the main street, except for two new developments in the 1960s, and is known as 'long-low lying-lazy Lyddington'.

Many of the buildings are made of local red sandstone quarried about two miles away at Stoke Dry quarries.

115

Lyddington village green

The church of St Andrew is one of great beauty. It has a very unusual altar table completely surrounded by communion rails which are dated 1653. Music was provided up to 1875 by a church orchestra made up of two violins, a cello, bugle, double bass and a trombone. A barrel organ was installed in 1876, but was quickly replaced by a hand-pumped manual organ in 1879.

There is a large building to the north of the church, the Bede House. The present building is one of the finest examples of 15th century domestic architecture in the country. It has been said that Henry VIII and Katherine Howard stayed here when travelling from Lincoln to London. It was last occupied in the early 1930s. Since then it has been lovingly restored to its former glory. This has been a long process taken over many years and it is now in the custody of English Heritage. In the Park Field, east of the Bede House, there are a series of fish ponds which once supplied the kitchen with fresh fish.

There were five public houses in use, the Lord Roberts (now 4 Main Street), the Pied Calf (13 Main Street), the Swan coaching inn (36 Main Street), The Olde White Hart and the Marquis of Exeter. The latter two still exist. The Swan Inn was very popular before the turnpike road between Uppingham and Caldecott was constructed because the then main road passed through Lyddington.

Stoke Road, off the green, was known as Pig Lane, here pigs were penned prior to being sold on the village green.

There were five laundries, which did the laundry for Uppingham

School, eleven working farms (there are now two), seven shoemakers and stonemasons, three tailors, carpenters and grocers, four bakers, two blacksmiths, cattle dealers and shepherds, and three shops. The village now has none of these, except for a small shop and post office.

There used to be a village cross on the green which was removed by drunken navvies who were building the new road from Uppingham to Caldecott. It was deposited in a local builder's yard for many years, before being reinstated with great celebrations in 1930, with several artefacts of the time being buried underneath.

The Gleaning Bell was sounded at 8 am and 5 pm during harvest time for the locals to go into the fields to 'glean' the 'left over' corn. The Passing Bell was rung until the late 1950s.

A very active village school closed in the late 1960s and the village is now very much a 'commuter village'.

Lyndon

Some years ago the roads entering the village were lined with lime trees. Ash and oak now take their place, although there are a few splendid limes still in the centre of the village.

This is a tiny village with approximately 38 houses. Cottages which were once occupied by farm and estate workers are now holiday or 'short-let' homes. Most of the village remains in the hands of the Conant family. Sir John Conant lives in Lyndon Hall, a grand William and Mary house set in beautiful grounds.

The church is a mere stone's throw away and dates back to the 13th century. Like the village it is small but beautiful, with a seating capacity of about 60. Not many of these seats are filled at regular services but Christmas is the exception. There is also a village hall, which was built in 1922. Like the church it was better attended some 30 years ago. A whist drive is held most Friday nights, but it is seldom used for a village 'get-together'. At one time it was open most evenings for the pleasures of darts, billiards and dances.

Lyndon must have been quite a busy village years ago. Evidently there were five tenant farmers. Most of the surrounding fields were down to grass for cattle grazing, with neatly cut hedges to separate them. Now the hedges have gone, and there are extensive fields of corn and rape, all maintained by one farmer.

Thomas Barker, who was born at Lyndon Hall in 1722, was a pioneer in scientific weather observation. His journals recorded weather and other interesting topics, bee keeping and agriculture.

Medbourne 🌿

Medbourne is a very pretty village of ironstone and brick houses spread along both sides of a small brook which drains into the river Welland. There has been a settlement at this point since Roman times but the oldest existing house is the manor house, which dates from the 13th century.

The village has changed very little in appearance in the last 100 years except for some new building on the roads leading into the centre. Features of the village are the many mature trees which form a beautiful backdrop in spring and summer and the medieval pack horse bridge leading to the church.

The major change to village life was during the late 1800s when the branch railway line was built. From being a small insular village consisting of farmers and farm workers, a miller, baker, weaver, brewer and builder plus their various helpers and families, the population was suddenly increased by the influx of 'navvies' and their families, which caused some friction with the locals.

Another change at about the same period was the moving of the Fernie Hunt kennels to the village by Sir Bache Cunard, the master and owner of Nevill Holt Hall, which was formerly owned by the Nevill family from 1414 until 1868. The hunt servants were housed in cottages built by Sir Bache Cunard on Manor Road and the kennels were built alongside. The stables were also built at the bottom of the village on Ashley Road.

An odd tale of this time tells of the 'drumming out' of a local schoolmaster. Apparently the schoolmaster's wife was confined with the birth of a child and the man had been paying attention to his fellow teacher. The local people had taken offence at this and men from the stables made a straw effigy of the man which they carried in procession, beating on pans and metal lids to create a great noise, down to the recreation field, where they burnt it on a bonfire. The schoolmaster left the village soon after.

Now most people work away from the village including many women, so during the day the village is probably quieter than it used to be. The farms do not need as many workers as before and the school has now closed so the children leave in the early morning and do not return until mid-afternoon. The meeting places remain as the village shop, the church, village hall and, of course, the two remaining public houses.

A story of Medbourne would not be complete without mention of the 'Bottle Kicking' – it dates back at least 500 years. Before the enclosure of the Hallaton fields in 1770, the land where the event takes place was called Crop Leys, the rector of Hallaton receiving all rents and profits from this land on condition that he provided two hare pies, two dozen penny loaves and a quantity of ale to be scrambled for on Easter Monday after a service at the church. The event still draws large crowds to watch and to try their luck on either side, although it mostly falls on the young and not-so-young local men to uphold the honour of their villages.

Morcott 🦜

Morcott lies in the Wrangdyke Hundred of Rutland. This village of some 300 inhabitants is situated just off the A47 midway between Leicester and Peterborough. It is easily located by its famous landmark – a restored windmill, which stands majestically on the ridge above the south east edge of the village.

In bygone days there were a number of farms around the parish, some employing up to 15 men. The hooves of the farm horses were tended by the village blacksmith, the last member of the trade retiring in the 1930s, while further up the same road were the premises of the village carpenter cum wheelwright cum undertaker. Few farms remain today, their stone barns and buildings having been converted into private houses.

A number of the older buildings show the prosperity of the village in the 17th and 18th centuries. Priests House dates from 1627, and the manor house from 1687. Morcott Hall was the home of the Fydell Rowleys from around the end of the 18th century. It was said that when the squire walked in his gardens, the curtains at the manor house next door had to be drawn. The Hall has been the site of a private boarding school since the early 1940s. The rectory was built in 1830. There used to be a bakery at the edge of the village which cooked the Sunday joints for many families.

Gilson's almshouses were founded in 1612 – these have since been altered and reduced in number.

There was a time when the spiritual needs of the villagers were catered for by two chapels (Wesleyan and Baptist) and the church of St Mary the Virgin. The Wesleyan chapel is now privately owned while the Baptist chapel has been converted into the village hall. The church is the most complete Norman one in Rutland. Originally it consisted of a small nave and chancel, and the north and south aisles were added around 1150 and 1200.

In the late 19th century the village boasted five inns, of which only the

White Horse remains today. At Christmas the rent dinner was held in the Crown, when tenants would pay the second half year's rent to the squire, and the vicar collected his tithes. Morcott Feast was held annually with coconut shies, roundabouts, greasy pole climbing (for a pig) and dancing in the evening. Alas, this custom has long since lapsed.

Nailstone

A quiet, sleepy village, Nailstone stands high on the edge of the coalfield in the Hundred of Sparkenhoe, several miles from the now exhausted pits, surrounded by sweeping plough and grasslands, drawn into the 20th century courtesy of the M1 a few miles away on the edge of Charnwood Forest, and the M42 on the other side of Bosworth battlefield. A network of footpaths fan out over the fields, providing pleasant walks through meadows garlanded with wildflowers, alongside rambling streams.

The church dominates the green, encircled by Main Street and Church Road, where old cottages and modern dwellings, including the post office/shop blend harmoniously together, shaded by magnificent horse chestnut trees.

Sadly, the wood mentioned in the Domesday Book, then three furlongs by two furlongs, has now been reduced to a fringe of trees surrounding the pond near the old colliery. It is a favourite fishing haunt for locals.

Both pubs hold Gala Days, fetes, etc to raise money for charity, but in 1900 the landlord of the Bull's Head was also the local undertaker, and had a saw pit behind the pub where he made coffins, whilst the landlord of the Queen's Head was the local butcher, and had a slaughteryard behind the pub.

Two cottages next to the Queen's Head were built with two front doors in 1863 by eccentric Mr Gardener from Grange Farm (known as Bacon Hall to the staff due to their monotonous menu of bacon).

The course of history might have been changed one fateful day in 1745 when the Young Pretender, Prince Charles Stuart, and his Highlanders, having swept through England only to falter at Derby, rode to Elm Tree Farm to see the Knowles family to ascertain what support to expect from the area. The decision to retreat was made there. The head of the Knowles family was arrested for high treason, and condemned to hang, but later received a Royal Pardon. A goblet, known as the Stuart Cup was in the possession of the Knowles until the turn of the century, and was used to toast 'The King over the Water' at Jacobite meetings held in the dining room at the farm.

The great elm tree, which for centuries dwarfed the crossroads, was said to mark the most southerly point reached by Bonnie Prince Charlie, and the story was that should the tree fall no more babies would be born in the village. In the 19th century workers from Earl Howe's estate came to fell the tree, but it was saved by a local farmer's wife. Unfortunately it succumbed to nature in September 1962 and fell in a storm. But happily the prophecy remains unfulfilled and there is a new thriving school today, although the old National school built by Earl Howe in 1828 is now a private house.

All Saints church is 13th century, its 120 foot broach spire dominating the landscape. An ancient bier at the back of the church is dated 1664. Sergeant of the Pantry under four Tudor Kings and Queens, Thomas Corbett of Barton was buried here in 1586, and his memorial is well worth reading.

Nanpantan 🐿️

At the beginning of the 20th century Nanpantan, 300 ft above sea level and about two and a half miles west of Loughborough, consisted of the Hall, a mission church, a day school and about 20 cottages. In spite of the saying that an old man toiling up the hill said to his wife, 'Nan Pant On!', or the myth that a sailor returning from travels in the China Seas named his house, 'Nan Pan Tan', the logical derivation of the name seems to be 'Pantain' from the Anglo-Saxon word meaning enclosure. Part of the map of Charnwood Forest dated 1754, actually shows the position of 'Nan's Pantain'.

The parish boundary map of 1936 is vastly different to Nanpantan today. Some of the farms have disappeared to make way for housing. Burleigh Hall, which was fortified during the Civil War and held for the Royalists, was purchased by Loughborough College in 1949 – later, in 1967, it received its University Charter – and little remains of the former estate.

The Church of England mission church, 'St Mary's in Charnwood', is a small but well-constructed building of local stone. The war memorial, near the entrance is rather unusual in that it is a single large block of natural Charnwood granite. The granite outcrops are a feature of the area, especially Beacon Hill on the periphery of Nanpantan, from the top of which are splendid panoramic views overlooking superb woodland and heath with gleaming reservoirs like miniature lakes.

Nearby is Whittle Hill, internationally famous for its 'hone' stones, until the import of carborundum from America. Known as Charnley Forest stones, they were formed by a layer of volcanic dust and are amongst the oldest in the forest. No doubt there are still old craftsmen who treasure their Whittle Hill stones. In 1949 the old quarry chimney from the boiler house was still standing behind the Whittle Hill farm.

Although the precise date of foundation is unknown, Holy Well Haw existed as a hermitage before 1180 and was a 'hospitium' for wayfarers crossing the forest. Today the farm is known as Holywell Farm and still retains the Gothic doorway.

All the trees had been sold before Moat Farm (mentioned in the Domesday Book) came under the hammer when the Beaumanor estate was sold, but Mrs Allesbrook, the owner, managed to save two oaks and an ash tree. The moat, giving the farm its name, still exists in good condition on two sides of the garden. Beacon Lane which passes through the fields of Moat Farm, is thought to have been a track from the Roman camp on the Beacon to the tumulus at Dishley.

A popular sport in the 18th and early 19th centuries was that of trotting races, which were held on the dead straight, almost level, 'Charley Mile' road. Nanpantan still has close connections with horses and on Boxing Day the Forest Road is flanked with people from all over the county to watch the Quorn Hunt.

Now, near the end of the 20th century, Nanpantan is a far cry from the bustling village it once was. Intersected by a busy crossroads, and dominated by the Priory – an inn where golfers of repute quaff a well-earned drink after playing the 18 holes of the nearby famous Longcliffe golf course. Standing on the terrace of this Dutch-style building on a clear day, one overlooks the flat plains of the Soar valley and the thriving university and market town of Loughborough into which, in recent years, Nanpantan has been absorbed.

Narborough & Littlethorpe

Narborough, a village community in South Leicestershire, is situated in fairly low lying country to the north of the river Soar, Littlethorpe being on the other side of the river.

A Roman villa was unearthed on the site of the new school in Copt Oak Road and the finds were important enough to call in Leicestershire Museum Excavation Unit. The Roman road, Fosse Way, leaves the present Leicester to Coventry highway at a point near the Huncote Road turning and crosses hospital land.

About 1815 the majority of villagers were engaged in framework knitting. Old houses were adapted and new ones with special wide windows to light the frames were built by businessmen for the knitters and their families. Even the children worked. But with the invention of steam-powered wide frames and building of factories in Leicester and Hinckley, poverty threatened Narborough. Comparative prosperity returned to the village with the building of the railway in 1864 with a station at Narborough. This is when the large Victorian villas began to appear in Leicester road. These stood in one or two acres of land and they employed many servants, who mainly lived in Victoria Street in what became known as the 'New Houses'.

In 1968 the Beeching axe fell and Narborough station was closed. It was mainly through the efforts of Mr 'Dai' Williams and the Parish Council, also Blaby RDC, that it was reopened on the 5th January 1970. This was a big day for Narborough.

There are two very old pubs in Narborough. Narborough Hotel is a very old coaching house and was once part of the property which went with Narborough Hall. There are characteristic stone footings on the older buildings, as the Bell, whose exact age is not known. It was once very small and was surrounded by cottages. Littlethorpe used to have several very old pubs, two of which, still going strong, are the Old Inn and the Plough.

There used to be thatched cottages all along the main street and at Littlethorpe, some of these were demolished as recently as the 1960s.

All Saints church goes back to the 12th century, but the 10th century tombstone found near the present churchyard must surely mean that a wooden building once stood where the present stone built church now stands.

Narborough Hall was probably built about 1500 and is a very interesting old house. The Yeoman's House, Littlethorpe, dates from the 16th century.

Newbold, Coleorton 🐑

Situated in north-west Leicestershire, you won't find Newbold appearing on any calendars or picture postcards. Most of the village is post-war, formed around a scattering of farms and cottages that were originally a hamlet of neighbouring Worthington.

It has a school, a pub and a former vicarage and these together with a couple of timber framed farmhouses and the original hamlet cottages are Newbold's main claims to antiquity.

What would a villager of the past think of Newbold today? Would they look in vain for 'Snip' Stewart's stores at the junction of School Lane and Melbourne Road? Remembering when the shop used to open at 4.30 am to serve the miners their 'thick' and 'thin' twist (tobacco), polo mints and carbide for their lamps as they joined their shift across the road at New Lount Colliery. Would they marvel at the silence and desolation that now surrounds this self same mine since its closure and demolition in 1968? Like that of its brother employer, the pipeworks on Worthington Lane.

Passing along School Lane and into Worthington Lane it may be thought that progress has not been too kind to Newbold. The Cross Keys has long ago lost its thatch as have, one by one, the other older properties. George Crabtree, who buried so many of Newbold's residents, is himself buried along with the business he ran. Even Crabby's pond that bears his name is filled in and grassed over.

The well, at the junction of Ashby Road and School Lane, has met a similar fate. It exists now only in local vocabulary, though surprisingly enough, the Bush well, on Melbourne Road, is still extant and is used regularly to water sheep in nearby fields.

As would be expected from a mining village, Newbold has had its tragedies, such as the case of Edward Williams, who survived the horrors of war only to become the first miner killed in the newly opened New Lount Colliery. Or the 'black damp' that seeped through Newbold Glory killing amongst others, five members from the same family.

The lovely old bluebell woods that once surrounded the village have now fallen victim to the open cast mining and sadly are mere shadows of their former selves.

As a small consolation, however, the pit spoil heap which once towered over the village like a malignant blister, is now a green and pleasant hill, landscaped and set with trees and containing the remnants of Spring Wood pool.

Newbold Verdon

The name Newbold Verdon is of Norman origin. It relates to one Bertram de Verdun, who had the tenure of the village in the 12th century. The prefix Newbold means new-built or new buildings. Over the years Newbold Verdon has grown into a large thriving village, not picturesque, somewhat scattered, but for friendly character it takes some beating.

Gone are the days when half the village had the surname of Statham and you had to add a nickname (Whiskey Statham esq, Main Street) if you wanted to be sure a letter was delivered to the correct person. But the older inhabitants mix well with the new and so the village boasts a variety of clubs.

A church was first built probably in the late 12th or early 13th century. St James' church was rebuilt in 1898 in celebration of Queen Victoria's Diamond Jubilee, at the estimated cost of £2,786. There was not enough money to build a tower at the time, so this was finally put up and dedicated in 1960.

One village character who became important during the Second World War as an ARP warden was Walter Preston. His job was to blow his whistle whilst riding around the dark village streets on his trusty bicycle, first to warn of an approaching air raid, then to blow the 'all clear'. He and the headmaster of the primary school ran the local 'Dad's Army', with the headmaster as Chief Fire Officer.

One of their joint manoeuvres was to see how long it would take to put out a large fire, so one was built and lit during daylight hours on the Dragon field. By the time Walter, cycling furiously round to collect the men together, actually had them on the spot, the fire had gone out! Only three bombs fell here during the whole war, so perhaps speed and efficiency were not needed to any great effect. After the war Walter was Chairman of the Parish Council along with some of his fellow ARP men. They helped the village expand with the first two large housing estates. They also purchased the playing field, making friendship and sport the heart of the Newbold Verdon of today.

Main Street, Newbold Verdon

Newton Harcourt 🐾

The history and development of Newton Harcourt is inevitably linked with nearby Wistow Hall, whose owners possessed all the land surrounding the village in the late 18th century. The parish is still named Wistow-cum-Newton Harcourt, with the mother church at Wistow and the chapel at ease in Newton.

The oldest building in the village is the manor, once a dower house, with pre-Elizabethan origins. St Luke's church lies opposite the manor. It has a Norman tower, but the body of the church was built in the 19th century. One day, when Sir Henry Halford was sitting at his window, he noticed that the weather vane on the church tower was not turning, so he took pot shots at it with his gun to make it spin. The holes can be seen today.

Further up in the village stands Octagon cottage. As its name implies, it has eight walls and dates from the mid 18th century when it was used as a toll house, where drovers stopped to pay a toll for watering their cattle and sheep in the nearby stream. The cottage has been divided and now houses two families.

It is very hard to imagine Newton Harcourt before enclosure in 1773, but at this time a ten acre piece of land, to be known as the Poor's Land, was put in trust for the benefit of the poor. Divided into allotments, the rent was used to buy clothing, but nowadays the income from the one tenant is given to OAP's each Christmas. Undoubtedly, one of the chief factors in modernising the landscape was the now peaceful Grand Union Canal, which cuts straight through the lower part of the village. Fifty years later the railway was built alongside the canal and now carries main line trains between Sheffield and London.

Despite these two major disturbances to the surrounding countryside, farming continued to be the main occupation in Newton. There were five farms forming the nucleus of the village. In 1814 cottages were built for the farm workers and included a blacksmith's, a bakehouse, a laundry and a temporary morgue! Suicides were apparently a common occurrence here with the close proximity of canal and railway as the means of opportunity.

These buildings formed the Square, at the end of which was the public house, first called The Bull and later The Recruiting Sergeant. A notable incident occurred in 1870 with a shoot-out between gamekeepers from Wistow and poachers. One gamekeeper, Thomas Monk, was killed and as a result the pub lost its licence because the incident was blamed on drunkenness. The building continued as an off-licence for a further 100 years and is now a family home, as are the other cottages in the Square.

Water supply had always been a problem for the village. Each farm had its own pump. It was not until the mid 1950s that mains water was connected. The first private house was built in 1961 and since then 20 more have been erected. The village has changed radically in those years. There is only one working farm now and most residents commute to Leicester.

Newtown Linford 🦡

As you approach this charming village from Leicester via Anstey there is a fine view of Bradgate Park and Cropston reservoir to your right. This medieval deer park was formerly the property of the Grey family. It still contains the ruins of an early example of a brick, unfortified country house, the childhood home of Lady Jane Grey, who became Queen of England for nine days in 1553. When the estate was sold in the 1920s Charles Bennion of British United Shoe Machinery Company bought the park and presented it to the people of Leicester and Leicestershire, who have continued to enjoy its spectacular scenery of old oaks and craggy outcrops of ancient rock.

The medieval church by the park gates is dedicated to All Saints. It is built of Charnwood Forest stone and roofed in local Swithland slate, as are many of the village houses. This same slate marks the older graves. The Gothic windowed Sunday school was built by the Earl of Stamford, lord of the manor, in 1822. It housed the village school before the present one was built almost a century later. Beyond the church lies the cricket field, one of the most attractive in the county.

For those interested in architecture, the village provides several examples of both timber framed and stone built dwellings, roofed in thatch or slate. Behind the 20th century facade of the Bradgate Hotel lies an older village inn, where carriers used to refresh themselves and change their horses. Until the Second World War many of the cottages provided teas for visitors and the village still has a variety of places to eat. Opposite the hotel the group of buildings round the courtyard was once a farm with a sheep dip. Now there are only two farms but there were ten at the break up of the Bradgate estate in 1925. At that time the entire village was sold and happily many tenants were able to buy their own homes.

At the junction of Markfield Lane and Main Street was once a ford, from which Newtown Linford derived its name. The river Lin rises beyond Ulverscroft and flows parallel to the Main Street before passing through Bradgate Park and into Cropston reservoir.

Lenthill Farm, recently a working farm, was at one time the village inn known as the Bucks Head or the Horns Tavern, under which name it played an important part in a local custom. Until 1870 Newtown Linford was part of an ecclesiastical oddity, the Peculiar of Groby. Every few years the Peculiar held a court in Newtown Linford church to deal with people who had failed to pay their fines for offences like ringing the bells without first removing their coats or spurs! At the end of the Court the company processed up the village street to the Horns Tavern. There they had a dinner, for which Lord Stamford always gave a pike from Groby Pool and a buck from Bradgate Park.

North Kilworth

The next time you are labouring down a lorry-filled A427 between Lutterworth and Market Harborough, instead of ignoring the blur which is North Kilworth, turn off the road and be prepared for a surprise.

You will enter a compact village built on two sides of a valley where the interlinking roads form geometric patterns. None of the old village streets have street name signs. This is a village of predominantly red brick walls, a mixture of artisans' cottages and handsome large houses, interspersed with modern additions. Many of these directly front the road and between them you will see yards and paddock areas. You may still see sheep, horses and donkeys grazing near the middle of the village.

At the top of a hill you will find a 12th century church of Early English architectural style. The Jacobean pulpit is known as the Armada pulpit as it is made of Spanish oak. The name of Archbishop Laud is proudly displayed on the list of rectors of this parish. Here too you first notice the name of Belgrave, landowners here for several centuries.

The village probably developed from an Anglo-Saxon settlement and 'Chevelsworde' was its name in the Domesday Book. In the 19th century the building of the canal and railway brought in new and varied employment. Coal was brought along the canal by barge, bagged, weighed and sold round the village on horse and dray. At the turn of the century many men were employed at George Ball's Royal Implement Works making carts and wagons and the family firm still functions as a wheelwrights.

Villagers could once refresh themselves after work at any one of five pubs but only two remain. There is a village shop, a post office and two petrol stations. There was, not so long ago, a village carrier who visited neighbouring market towns on set days with a horse and cart carrying out commissions for villagers.

If you associate North Kilworth with glowing colours and beautiful scents you must have visited the rose garden run by Mr Douglas Gandy, a rose grower and propagator of international reputation.

Norton-juxta-Twycross

Norton-juxta-Twycross is about a mile north of Twycross. It was granted a Royal Charter in AD 951 by the Saxon King Eldred, and it was then called Northton. By the 16th century its name had changed to Hogges Norton. The parish was enclosed about 1749. It is a small village of 50 houses, four farms, a public house – the Moores Arms, the post office, and an agricultural manufacturer.

The church of Holy Trinity was built in the 12th century. The spire was removed in 1890. The church has a barrel organ which three ladies of the village were instrumental in restoring. It is now in perfect working order and the congregation sometimes uses it when there is no organist for Sunday services.

There is an ancient tombstone in the churchyard dated 1715, to one John Worthington in which the letters all run together, with no spaces between the letters and some letters back to front.

As Hogges Norton the village was the inspiration for the old radio show by Gillie Potter in the late 1940s, with his humorous monologues about the characters and goings on in a farming village.

Twycross Zoo house was the rectory to Norton church and was built in 1851. It is now the main building at Twycross Zoo, which is in the parish of Norton-juxta-Twycross.

The village hall, which is owned by the villagers, was erected by Jack Lea, a carpenter from the village, just after the end of the First World War, in 1920, as a memorial to the men of Norton whose names are on a plaque inside the hall. Joe and Udi Marshall kept the village blacksmith's shop and saddlery and their wives looked after the pub. There was a village shop and post office, and a sweet shop, the sweet shop kept by a Mr North. Today there is just a post office. The village school was closed in the 1940s.

It is still quite a close knit community with the old village spirit still present.

Old Dalby 🦋

Old Dalby is placed in a fold of land below a steep escarpment of the Wolds – hence its real name is Wold Dalby or Dalby on the Wolds.

The hall and much of the land was once owned by the Knights Hospitaller. In the 1920s and 1930s Old Dalby Hall was still in full existence with a squire and his wife. Many staff were employed – village folk mainly, butler, footmen, cooks, housemaids, kitchen maids, estate agents, gardeners, chauffeur, grooms, cowmen (with a herd of pedigree Jersey cows), also men in charge of thoroughbred horses. Electricity was made on the premises (the engine house is now a bungalow). Now the hall is converted into private residences and the stables into a nursing home.

In the churchyard near the gate is a headstone, moved from the back of the church, of one, Edward Purdey, aged 35 years who died in 1743. The inscription reads:

'Through a woman I received the wound which quickly brought my body to the ground. It's sure in time that she will have her due. The murdering hand God's vengeance will pursue. The debt I ow'd that caused all the strife was very small to cost me my sweet life. She threatened to give me a mark and made her cause look very dark'. The story is that Edward, after drinking at the Durham Ox at Six Hills, was unable to pay ½d for his beer. The landlady turned her dog on him, which proved rabid and poor Edward died of rabies. The word halfpenny is also written on the stone in small writing.

There were two pubs in the village, one is now a private residence but the Crown Inn is now a popular centre for people travelling from the city for a meal in the country. Outside the Crown is a small green, originally a duck pond, which was filled in at the WI's behest and on which they planted a tree.

The village often became snowbound. The village men rode cart horses to Wymeswold (six miles) to the nearest baker to collect bread. Now snowploughs operate quickly to clear the road.

Osgathorpe 🦋

The small peaceful village of Osgathorpe lies tucked in a fold of hills in the north-west of the county, easily missed by passing travellers. It has often been said that anyone coming here either lives in the village or is lost. But despite its small size Osgathorpe has a history dating back well before the Domesday Book in which it is mentioned. Clues to its origin lie with the ford and spring, still used for drinking water, and the nearby remains of a quarry at Barrow Hill. Several of the houses in the village are built of local stone.

The church of St Mary the Blessed Virgin lies at the heart of Osgathorpe. Its main part was built in 1204 with later additions, including a tower and vestry, erected in 1931. The churchyard contains an interesting five-sided sundial. Next to the church is a fine example of a Tudor timber framed yeoman's house, now known as Manor Farm, which is reputed to be one of the oldest houses in the village.

Set slightly back from the road, and at right angles to the Old Rectory, is The Residence, originally an almshouse for clergymen's widows. This house, together with neighbouring Harley House and the Old Grammar School, was built in the 1680s with a generous bequest from Thomas Harley, a former Lord Mayor of London. The school is now the village hall but, like the schoolmaster's house and almshouse, retains many of its original architectural features. Thomas Harley had his country home at Osgathorpe Hall, another beautiful building which stands on a hill at the edge of the village.

Industrial prosperity passed Osgathorpe by when the ill-fated Old Forest Canal failed to hold water. Nor did the railways or coal mining affect the village as it did the surrounding area. So Osgathorpe today is still a very rural place with several working farms in its centre. People in the village now have a wide variety of occupations ranging from farming to the space industry, from mining to fine arts. Nowadays its only amenity is a part time post office but there used to be several shops, including a blacksmith and wheelwright. However, there are two public houses and a third on the edge of the village.

Owston 🐑

Owston (pronounced Ooston) appeared in the 1086 Domesday Book as Osulvestone and was listed as having a population of 22. Situated in the heart of the East Leicestershire 'highlands' on clay uplands rising to 700 feet, the village was favourable sited on what must have been well established trading and droving routes in medieval times. Robert Grimbald, one of Henry II's justices, and the principal tenant of Owston, founded an Augustinian abbey of 13 canons on the site in 1161.

When it was dissolved by Henry VIII in 1536, only the abbot and six canons were in residence. Today, the only tangible reminders of the abbey's existence are terraced fields to the west of the village indicating walls, boundary banks and former fish ponds. There is also the church, dedicated to St Andrew, which possibly represents the original chancel and north chapel of the ancient abbey church.

Over the ensuing centuries Owston has remained a purely agricultural community which, until the 20th century, was virtually self-sufficient. Census returns reveal a population in the mid 19th century of 180, three times today's numbers, housed in accommodation which is essentially unchanged today. To serve the village there were at one time two pubs, a grocer's shop, and a post office-cum-general store. Besides the normal agricultural occupations of grazier, carter, dairyman, carrier and groom, the census returns also list a dressmaker, tailor, wheelwright, blacksmith, woodman, carpenter, boot repairer, carriage builder, gamekeeper and several domestic servants such as cooks, housekeepers and housemaids who would, presumably, have mainly been employed at outlying farms.

Schooling was self-sufficient too. In 1856 the Palmers of Withcote Hall established a village school (now used as a barn) and for nearly a hundred years up to as many as 40 children received primary education in a single class under one schoolmistress. Falling numbers brought an end to the school in 1946.

The coming of the railway, as late as 1872, had less impact on this self-sufficient society than elsewhere. Principally this was because the nearest station was at Tilton, two miles distant by heavily gated roads. Although the railway enabled farmers to distribute milk and cheese further afield, and facilities for transporting sheep and cattle were improved, the railway's influence remained comparatively limited and short-lived and, after only 84 years of operation, the line was closed in 1956.

Even without any form of shop or the unifying influence of a resident priest, postmistress or publican, the church and the village hall provide a nucleus of sorts and Owston's small population ensures a genuine corporate identity which assumes concrete shape at functions such as Harvest Supper, 5th November, and the Christmas carol service.

Peatling Magna

Peatling Magna is one of the oldest settlements in Leicestershire, believed to date from the first century AD. It appeared in the Domesday Book as 'Petlinge'. The medieval village was probably more widely-spread, over a slightly different area from today, judging from house-platform sites on the edges of the present village.

The church is 12th century, with a 14th century spire, and contains several old tombs, mostly of the Jervis family, lords of the manor for some 200 years from Elizabethan times. A Jacobean memorial on the chancel wall commemorates a William Jervis who was 'High sheriff of this Shire' when he died in 1618. One daughter of the house was Dr Samuel Johnson's 'Beloved Tetty', whom he married in 1735, but there is no record of them ever coming here.

Although the total number of residents has varied very little over the years, the lifestyles have, of course, changed considerably. Gone are the wheelwright and carpenter, the blacksmith, the butcher – villages are no longer self-sufficient as they once had to be. Car-owning now is a 'must', especially as there are no shops nearer than two and a half miles from Peatling Magna, just a part time post office and a pub. There are still several farmers in the community, but most people in work commute each day.

The houses in the village are mostly 19th and 20th century buildings, and a few of 18th century date, though some have older foundations. Since the Second World War, there has been infilling on houseplots, but no 'estate' development as such. Main sewerage did not arrive until 1981.

The fields in the parish are largely arable, with grazing for sheep and some cattle, plus a few horses. A small stream winds its way through fields to the east of the village. Along some of its length grow alders and large willows, and on its banks there are signs of a medieval mill, probably for cloth-fulling.

Peckleton

Peckleton is a Saxon village, referred to in the Domesday Book as 'Peckintone'. It is a small rural village set in the heart of the Leicestershire countryside, still more or less the same size as it has always been.

The passing years have seen many changes in village life, the cottages which housed the miners, factory and farm workers are now almost gone. Shops, a brickyard, wheelwrights, tailors, carpenters were all situated within the village and also a Wesleyan chapel. It was a very different scene from today. Nowadays the village is inhabited by people who earn their living in many different ways – some still from the land, the coal mines, the inn, from the professions, commerce, industry and the arts.

It was a haven for evacuees during the Second World War. British and American soldiers, and later German prisoners, were in a camp here.

Pilots were trained in Tiger Moths in the parish. Altogether it was a very lively place.

The school was built in 1877 and closed in 1961. The Duck Paddle Lane, now Brook Lane, was prone to floods and the Brown Horse Inn being at the bottom of the hill was once vacated by a man in an old tin bath.

The church of St Mary Magdalene is the most important building in Peckleton. It has a Kempe window and a Norman font. Thomas Boothby Esq gave six bells and the communion silver to the church and his remains are interred under the belfry. He was believed to be the first man to start a pack of hounds in Leicestershire. There is a Druids Oak at the south side opposite the church gate where it is said a soldier is buried.

There is now one public house, no shops and the rectory has been sold. Whist drives, fetes and a three day church festival take place during the year but with a different pattern than in the past involving a different kind of community. The custom of the Plough Service has been revived to bless the work of the farmer.

Pickwell ✤

The village of Pickwell stands on one of the old prehistoric highways. The Domesday Book of 1086 describes the village as active in agriculture, a large portion being under the plough. In addition there was a mill, which was situated on the stream, and this gave Pickwell its importance.

The building of the Norman church was commenced in the 12th century on the old Saxon church site. From about 1225 it was found necessary to enlarge the church on the north side of the nave and in about 1300 a similar enlargement was made on the south side. The south aisle is particularly splendid with buttresses and niches. The present building was completed in the 15th century with the building of the Perpendicular tower. John Cave was vicar of Pickwell at the time of the Civil War. As a Royalist he suffered much at the hands of the Roundheads. His son attained distinction after the Restoration in 1660 and became Canon of Windsor and chaplain to Charles II.

In 1835 the school in the village was built by subscription and later enlarged. In 1922, 24 children were attending the school. Several years later the senior pupils were transferred to Melton Mowbray and in 1933 the 35 juniors then attending were transferred to Somerby and Pickwell school was closed. The property was transferred to the residents of the village to become the present village hall.

The main activities of the parish continue to be agricultural, in arable and mixed farming.

Pilton ﵟ

Pilton is a tiny village four miles north-east of Uppingham, standing on high ground, south of the river Chater. It is probably Rutland's smallest village. It is not a hamlet, for it has its own church – the pretty little 13th century church of St Nicholas. It was used as a school in 1584 and the glass windows suffered in consequence.

Some Roman and medieval remains have been found and as with so many Rutland villages, the pattern of ridge and furrow cultivation can still be seen. The Pilton side of the Chater valley with its small fields, many with dry stone walls, provides a contrast to the view over the Lyndon side of the valley with its prairie-like fields denuded of hedgerows.

Nowadays there are only seven inhabited houses, two of which are farms and in 1989 there were twelve inhabitants. In 1891 there were 46 people but the cottages in which they lived have entirely disappeared.

Most of the buildings are of local limestone but one or two are built of a noticeable rose coloured brick which was made locally. Ironstone quarries were opened in 1912 and a brickworks was set up for the building of railway bridges. In 1919 the Pilton Ironstone Railway was opened by Staveley Coal and Iron Company Ltd.

These industries no longer exist, the railway being closed in 1969. The quarry excavations are now used as landfill sites but traces of the old railway can be seen at the village crossroads.

Before 1900 the village had its own curate who resided in the rectory, now renamed Willaighby Cottage.

One of the oldest houses is Bay House Farm which dates back to the 17th century – travellers were able to change horses here until a serious fire wrecked all the stabling in 1860. Even in the coldest winter the horses could drink from the pond in the yard, which was said never to have frozen over.

There is no evidence of a village shop, although the thatched cottage on the Lyndon road is said to have been the village inn. The brawling and fighting among the railway workers building the line is said to have closed it. It was also reputed to be the hideaway of highwaymen, who preyed on travellers using the Great North Road.

One of the roads they used is now no more than a faint streak across the fields, visible only in winter.

Potters Marston

There is not much left of the village of Potters Marston; just about half a dozen houses, the Hall, which is now a farmhouse, and the church. In the Middle Ages it was quite a flourishing little village and it got its name because there was a pottery there. Earthenware pots which were made at the pottery have been found in various parts of Leicestershire. They were not elaborate items or very ornate ones, just ordinary cooking pots for household use. The remains of the pottery were excavated in the late 1940s.

The hall has had some of its panelling removed which was sold and sent to North America, but quite a lot of it still remains. In the hall grounds, which is also the farmyard, is the medieval dovecote.

The church must be one of the smallest in Leicestershire. It is just a rectangular building with no tower or steeple. In fact many people do not even know of its existence for you have to go through the farmyard to reach it. It is, however, still in use. There is a service there in the afternoon on the first Sunday in the month, and a carol service at Christmas.

Although Potters Marston is sometimes regarded as one of the deserted villages of Leicestershire it is still very much a living entity.

Preston

Preston, Rutland, is an attractive village lying on the main Uppingham to Oakham road. Many of the houses are built of local ironstone and in the rays of the evening sunshine take on a lovely mellow golden shade.

The church is a beautiful building mainly 14th and 15th century with a richly decorated Norman arch and a glorious east window. The manor house dates from the 17th century and Preston Hall also from this period, with additional wings added later.

There used to be six farmers and two smallholders in the village, one farmer also brewing his own beer and owning a threshing outfit. There were several tradesmen too, a baker, blacksmith, master thatcher, wheelwright and carpenter, butcher, tailor and two signalmen. There were only two commuters in those days, one by bicycle and the other on a motorbike, both going to work at Corby steelworks.

The cottages were occupied by grooms, gardeners and farmworkers. Everybody knew everyone else and there was a strong spirit of good neighbourliness throughout the village. There was a school, two shops and a post office, now sadly all gone.

The church choir of approximately 18 voices enjoyed an annual outing to the Choir Festival at Peterborough Cathedral. Rogationtide meant clergymen and choir going to farms, fields and allotments to ask God's blessing on the crops. Allotment holders would cease their work to join in the service, often joined by a bleat or bellow. All these occasions are now past and only one allotment holder remains.

Preston Feast was a highlight, the Sunday following 29th June. Sunday meant church, often followed in many homes by tea for visiting friends, the speciality being curd tarts, often baked in the bakehouse for 1d a dozen and fruit cakes for 2d. Sunday dinner could also be bought from the baker's wife for 2d each.

Preston and Ridlington Flower Show was formed in 1950 and has continued to thrive and enlarge. Classes for flowers, fruit and produce are well supported with photography and flower arrangements being later additions, which draw exhibitors from a wide area.

Preston is a neat and tidy village, thanks to the efforts of the residents, one in particular who mows the banks, which in spring are adorned with daffodils. Preston has won the tidy village contest several times.

Queniborough 🎋

Queniborough is located seven miles north-east of Leicester on the Melton Mowbray road and has a population of 2,400.

Over the years many Saxon items, broken tools and jewellery have been unearthed by local farmers. The village name has changed its spelling many times from 'Cuinburg', in the Domesday Book, to Queeniborough and finally Queniborough.

The main street in Queniborough retains the appearance of a country village and has many fine buildings. St Mary's church is a fine Gothic structure with a 13th century tower and 162 ft spire, containing six bells, four of which date back to 1619. The church also has a beautiful locally carved wooden screen and a pulpit made from old oak church pews.

The white thatched cottage in the centre of the village is one of the oldest, dating back to the 15th century. Its uses over the years have included a public inn, a blacksmith's, a cycle repair shop and in the early part of the 20th century it boasted its own petrol pump. Today it is a family home.

Today the village has two public houses: the Britannia Inn and the

Horse and Groom. At one time in the past the village boasted a minimum of seven drinking places. Approximately 100 years ago a tame bear was kept in the garden of the Britannia Inn. Her name was Fanny – she regularly escaped and went walking around the village.

The 20th century has seen many changes in the village, particularly in house building. The Ringway was built in the 1950s, a housing area in the shape of a ring. Two housing estates have been recently completed on the edge of the village, one of sheltered housing for the retired and the other of 70 executive houses.

One gentleman resident with a particularly interesting hobby, is a rail enthusiast and owner of the Queniborough Railway Museum. He has had to build a 40 ft extension onto his garage to house his collection. Such an enthusiast is he that he has a fully working signal and signal box in his garden.

In 1987/88 the dovecote was resited, with the help of young people on a youth training scheme. Originally sited in the grounds of Queni-borough New Hall, it now stands in a paddock behind the church, beautifully restored.

Historically a thriving farming community, Queniborough still has several farms in and around the village boundary. It was on one of these, Homestead Farm, that the Queniborough mystery arose. In the 1930s the skeleton of an unknown woman, believed to be about 200 years old, was dug up in one of the fields of Homestead Farm. What her body was doing there nobody is quite sure. Originally the site was the main road from Queniborough to Syston. Was foul play committed? We shall never know!

Quorn 🪶

Quorn is situated south of Loughborough and derived its name from the old English 'Cweordun' – quern stones which were mill stones used for grinding grain into flour and for sharpening swords.

The most famous connection with the village is the Quorn Hunt. Hugo Meynell, described as the father of English fox-hunting, was Master of Quorn Hunt for nearly 50 years. He lived at Quorn Hall, built on the banks of the river Soar, where he had extensive stables and kennels. Huntsmen riding with the Quorn Hunt brought a great deal of employment to the village. The smithy was responsible for shoeing the horses, while hostelries provided accommodation. Even today some of the street names are reminders of the great hunting days, Flesh Hovel Lane being the place where old horses were taken to the abattoir to be slaughtered. The meat was used to feed the hounds.

The village abounded with shops catering for all the needs of the local community. These included cobblers, producing hand-made shoes, tailors, milliners and saddlers. Even though the population was only about one third of today's figure, three bakers flourished and delivered bread. There were three or four milk delivery rounds with milk supplied direct from local farms. Cattle, sheep and pigs bought in Loughborough market were brought back to Quorn to be slaughtered.

In 1860 Wrights Factory, Quorn Mills took over the lace and cotton factory, to produce cords, braids and gussetings and during the First and Second World Wars the factory supplied much of the webbing equipment for the armed forces. Webbing is still produced in Quorn today, and this is still the major factory in the village. Some cottages in the village housed machines for sock and stocking making, and in the centre of the village a candle making factory was located in Tallow Fat Yard.

St Bartholomew's church of Norman origin is the local parish church and today the Methodists and Anglicans worship together. The church contains a side chapel belonging to the Farnham family, whose ancestors have lived in Quorn for over 700 years. There is also a Baptist chapel, the original building now converted into two cottages.

There is still a village green, through which grows an avenue of lime trees planted as a memorial to the American paratroopers stationed in the village during the Second World War.

The centre of the village has a listed building which was used as a lock-up in the 18th century.

The local butcher's with its attractive thatched roof, old stone cottages and a site still available for the wakes, all mean that in spite of extensive building on the outskirts, Quorn still retains its friendly, village charm.

Ratby 🌿

Ratby is a large village between the ancient forest of Charnwood and what was Leicester Forest, about five miles north-west of the City of Leicester. Since the time of the earliest settlement, the area has known Romans, Danes and Normans. The Romans left evidence of their presence at Burrough Encampment while the fine church tower is the legacy of those great builders, the Normans. In the 14th century new farmsteads were built, the most important of these being Old Hayes, a moated farmhouse south-west of Ratby.

In the church there is a monument to Sir Henry Sacheverelle, who in his will dated 19th September 1616, left £100 for the benefit of the poor of the parish. His trustees invested this in land at Botcheston and each Christmas a small sum from this trust is still distributed to a number of elderly and infirm in the parish.

The cottages were all clustered around the church and are there today, most having been sympathetically restored. This part of the village is now a conservation area. In the early 1860s Richardson's framework knitting factory at the foot of Stamford Street was established and here approximately 20 men were employed. The factory continues in use today. With the building of larger factories such as Tylers in Upper Stamford Street, later to become the Wolsey factory, the cottage framework knitting industry declined, although many villagers still work in factories in Leicester.

Ratby's growth continued with the coming of the Leicester to Swannington railway, this being the second railway to operate in the country. While the line was mainly concerned with the transport of minerals, eventually a passenger service was inaugurated. The old booking office is now incorporated in the Railway Inn. The village expanded rapidly, houses being built in Station Road and Stamford Street and men finding employment in the quarrying and coal mining industries. With the closure of Groby quarries and the gradual working-out of local pits only a few earn their livings in this way now.

Ratby has grown tremendously since the end of the Second World War. An engineering firm, a woodworking firm, Geary's the baker and a good selection of shops all provide employment for local people, but the majority commute to Leicester. Geary's were Champion Bakers of England for many years and long before people became diet and health conscious, Mr Sidney Geary was baking his famous Rearsby bread at the request of a Consultant at Leicester Royal Infirmary. This far-seeing doctor wished patients with dietary problems to be supplied with wholemeal bread.

In Station Road is the recently built Sports Club, with its logo of a crow, a reminder of the days when quantities of crow pie were eaten at the local hiring fairs.

Wakes week is held each May on the same land opposite the Plough Inn. Here also is the Statutes Craft (Stattie), the narrow path running from Stamford Street to the inn down which those presenting themselves at the hiring fairs would walk carrying the insignia of their trade. Other reminders of the past are the Mummers Play enacted in Ratby church on Plough Sunday and the Crow Pie Carnival.

140

Rearsby

It is difficult to visualise today, as one walks through Rearsby, that at one time it was quite an industrial community with various trades and crafts.

The church is situated in the middle of the village and is reached by crossing a well-known feature of Rearsby, Seven Arch Bridge. This was constructed in 1714 and legend has it that six men completed the work in nine days.

During the 1700s there were quite a few trades in the village. Records show that a whole family called Haynes were carpenters. Also at that time there was George Wollerton, a blacksmith and Mr Thomas Dawson, who must have been a brewer or innkeeper as he was often 'called upon to provide ale for parish functions'. A member of the Benskin family was a maltster. It is possible that Rearsby had one of Leicestershire's first framework knitters, as the Overseer's accounts have an entry 'for getting a frame for Thos Gilbert'.

One of the chief occupations between 1831 and 1844 was that of framework knitting, a cottage industry. There were 70 knitting frames in

Church of St Michael and All Angels, Rearsby

the village. Sadly all evidence has disappeared and it is not known which were the knitters' cottages.

Rearsby station was open in 1847. There were only five stationmasters between its opening and its closure in 1951. It is felt that a qualification must have been that one's surname must begin with an 'S' as their names were Sharp, Sugars, Shannon, Shelton and Slack.

There were eight farmers and graziers in the village in 1849, but 30 years later there were only six, one of whom was a farmer's widow.

In the 1900s there were even more changes in the village, shops sprang up and disappeared as the years passed. For instance, early in the century there was a greengrocer's, butcher's and cobbler's. A Mrs Dawson ran a haberdashery across the brook from Brookside. Boots and shoes were sold in a thatched shop on Brook Street – until it caught fire one Saturday morning. Eccentric Mrs Waite sold sweets, cigarettes and basic groceries from the cottage on the corner of Gaddesby Lane in the 1930s. The renowned Rearsby and Warden loaves were baked at Rearsby Mill by Warden and Matteson. Mr Geary bought the rights to these two loaves which still, to this day, are baked at Ratby Bakery.

The blacksmith managed to keep his business on Mill Road running by specialising in wrought iron work and repairing farm machinery. It was in 1939 that the Beagle Auster Aircraft opened on Gaddesby Lane.

Sadly there are only a few trades left now. There are three businesses, all in their third generation at Rearsby, Mr French the plumber, Mr Sherriff the builder and Mr Smith who runs the butcher's shop. There is still a post office and two public houses, the Wheel Inn and the Horse & Groom.

Ridlington

Once described as having the look of a village of the Welsh mountains, Ridlington perches on a windswept ridge overlooking the Chater valley. There can be few bleaker spots and it is certainly no place for people who feel the cold!

Cottages of local ironstone line the streets, snug beneath thatch or Collyweston slate. The 17th century manor house stands in the centre of the village. It was formerly the Old Hall and in 1605 was the home of Sir James Harrington, reputed to be responsible for organising the gunpowder and get-away horses for the Gunpowder Plotters.

The village no longer has a shop, public house or post office. The Noel Arms ceased trading as a pub in the late 1950s. The Bake House, which ceased trading in 1915, stands on Main Street. It once supplied the village with fresh bread. On Valentine's Day the baker used to make Plum Shuttles and a large basketful used to be taken to the school for distribution to the children.

The Old Post Office remains, a small thatched cottage at the end of Main Street. Before the penny post began in 1840 letters were delivered by hand by a messenger from Uppingham. Letters for the post had to be handed to the messenger as he walked round the village sounding a horn as he approached. After 1860 the postman, still on foot, would travel to Ridlington with letters, repair and mend shoes in his hut during the day, before returning to Uppingham in the evening with the Ridlington and area letters.

Ridlington Feast was held on the next Sunday after 22nd July and a week of cricket matches ensued, commencing with the traditional match against Wing. The players would be fiddled in and out and the visiting teams were entertained to tea/supper afterwards in the home players' houses. A cricket team now exists again and the cricket field is back in use on Saturdays and Sundays.

Overlooking the main street and village green is the church of St Mary and St Andrew. This was heavily restored in 1860 but a tympanum remains of the 12th century church. A case of old musical instruments can be seen at the back of the church.

In the past the village was mainly agricultural and men were engaged in all aspects of agriculture. Women too, were employed to help with potato setting and harvesting, hoeing of root crops and harvesting of the corn. Nowadays, with fewer farms, no dairy herds and large, more efficient farm machinery, far fewer people work on the farms but are now involved in employment in nearby Uppingham or Oakham.

Rothley 🖎

Rothley is half way between Leicester and Loughborough. The Red Lion Inn on the A6, a very old coaching inn, is also known as 'The Half Way House'. The village centre lies half a mile west of the A6.

Years ago the villagers worked at the local quarry at Mountsorrel, on the farms, for local builders (F. Sleath & Sons was established in 1870 and is still going) or in their cottages, frame knitting. Today with easy transport and access to motorways the occupations of 'Rothleyites' are varied, but some are still employed by the quarry and Rolls Royce works at Mountsorrel.

There are some very interesting buildings in Rothley. The church of St John the Baptist and St Mary the Virgin dates back to the 13th century and has a Saxon cross in the churchyard thought to date from the 8th century.

Rothley Court Hotel was once the home of the Knights Templar. Its 13th century chapel can still be viewed (by arrangement). It was at Rothley Court that Lord Macaulay was born on 25th October 1800. Lord Macaulay, together with Lord Wilberforce, is probably most famous for his work towards the abolition of slavery.

The Main Line Steam Trust runs steam trains between Loughborough and Rothley. Trains run on Saturdays and Sundays, Wednesdays in summer and school holidays. The station at Rothley is a great attraction for enthusiasts of all ages.

On the way to the church from Hall Fields Lane (once known as Rothley House Lane) there is a 'Dutchmen's Wall', so called because it was built by Dutchmen brought over in the 19th century to build defences against the sea on the East Coast. Also on this lane is Mr Bunney's smallholding, known locally as 'Rothley Safari Park'. Mr Bunney was also the name of the last town crier of Rothley, who up until 1922 would deliver important news items in the traditional manner.

There are many newcomers to the village and local industry is confined to two or three light engineering works and modern technology (computer) based firms. Rothley tends to be fragmented, so that meeting places become very important, but within the boundaries are a village hall, the Rothley Centre, the church, a baptist chapel, a Methodist chapel and a Roman Catholic church.

Saddington 🦜

Saddington stands on high ground some nine miles to the south-east of Leicester, midway between that town and Market Harborough. It has a current population of about 180, which is served by a church, a post office and a public house. The village is set in rolling countryside hunted by the Fernie and is the setting for the Hunt's cross country event each March.

As with many small villages there have been considerable changes over the last few years. A high proportion of the residents now find employment outside the village and increased mobility has brought about the demise of the village shop and school. The original post office, which was previously a chapel, is now a private residence, as is the old schoolhouse.

The village pump once stood at the bottom of Weir Road opposite the old blacksmith's cottage.

The village is mentioned in the Domesday Book under its original name of Setingtone. The first record of the present name occurs with the family of Robert de Sadington who resided here during the 14th century. It is from this period that parts of St Helen's church date. The building suffered considerable neglect during the 1600s but was gradually restored; notably by the architect Frederick Peck during the 1870s.

Part of the church is used as a village meeting place and is put to good use on summer Sunday afternoons when teas and refreshments are served. On fine days these are taken in the church grounds and these occasions are well supported by both villagers and passing motorists, walkers and especially cyclists.

To Leicestershire folk the name Saddington is synonymous with the reservoir which lies in the valley to the south of the village. The dam and reservoir were built during the 1790s to feed the canal running from Leicester up to Foxton Locks and beyond to Market Harborough.

The other notable canal feature connected with the village is the half mile long Saddington Tunnel, famed for its population of bats. It is reputed to be haunted. Records show that a large number of marine fossils were found during the construction of the tunnel and indeed such fossils can still be unearthed there.

Sapcote 🦔

Sapcote is a village ten miles from Leicester and four miles from Hinckley. Its boundaries are the Fosse Way on the Leicester side and the M69 motorway on the Hinckley side.

All Saints parish church dates from Norman times and the present building was probably erected on existing foundations some time between 1189 and 1307. Some say this may have been the second church, the first being named after St John the Baptist.

In 1837 an organ replaced an orchestra in leading the music. Apparently Sapcote church had a fine orchestra of violins, oboes, clarinets, bass fiddles and bassoons. Before this there was a band which comprised only reed instruments and a French horn. Music in Sapcote around 1800 was of a very high standard and when the local squire came to church he gave one of the congregation a guinea for the finest 'Amen' to the responses he said he had every heard.

The first Wesleyan chapel was built in 1805 at a cost of £470. A new

Wesleyan chapel was built in 1903. It is a fine building in Sapcote stone. The stone was given and quarried by members of the congregation. Extensive granite works employed a large number of the population. The granite was in great demand for road materials, kerbing and other purposes, and was said to be equal in quality to that found in any part of the United Kingdom.

Sapcote was a place of many springs and wells. The water from one special well passed through a bed of several veins of ironstone leaving a yellow deposit consisting chiefly of hydrated iron oxide. This yellow deposit gave the well its description and its rich sounding name, 'The Golden Well'. There was also a famous spring called 'Soap Well' which had remarkably soft water.

The first school in Sapcote was the Goodacre Charity School set up in 1694. Thomas Goodacre left a sum of money to be wisely invested in order to teach ten poor children to read. This building still remains and is one of only two thatched cottages left in Sapcote.

In 1847 almshouses were built to give accommodation for the benefit of five poor men, with money left by the Rev Stanley Burrough. Modernisation took place in 1972 and now there are four dwellings. Originally all the residents received a pension from the trustees. Nowadays maintenance payments are made by the residents to the trustees in order that the buildings may be cared for. How times change!

In the early 1900s Sapcote had over 200 knitting machines which made stockings. A good worker could make three stockings each day. Women sat on stools to make men's half-hose (socks). The children would wind the bobbins.

Sapcote was also known for its cheese making, and over 30 tons were taken to Leicester each year. There was much dairy farming done and many people were self-supporting. Everyone had a pigsty, poultry and ducks. In fact the last domestic cowshed has only recently been taken down to make way for more housing. Before the Second World War the majority of the men worked in the quarries.

The number of shops in the last 30 years has dwindled from over 20 to three, a post office, and a hairdresser's. There are two public houses, the Lord Bassett Arms and the Red Lion.

Scalford 🎷

Scalford, four miles north of Melton Mowbray, is mentioned in the Domesday Book and today has a population of approximately 400.

Before the First World War there were the usual varied occupations found in any country parish – farmers and coal merchants, brickmakers and wheelwright, a horse dealer, a carpenter, two blacksmiths, a lace agent, butchers, a florist and nurseryman, millers, a carrier, three bakers, dairy workers etc. Of these only one firm of bakers, a small number of farmers and the dairy workers remain now. Prior to 1939 Scalford Brickyard employed over 100 men making bricks and tiles and the brickyard chimney was a local landmark. A hundred cheeses are now made each day at The Dairy which employs ten people and has been winning prizes for Stilton Cheese since 1903.

Scalford is thought to have the only church in the country dedicated to St Egelwin, a Saxon saint, and he is supposed to be buried in the churchyard. The village is fortunate in that it has retained its rectory and the rector of Scalford with Wycombe and Chadwell is also rector of Goadby Marwood, Eastwell and Eaton. The village has also retained its school, built in 1861.

A railway station was built in 1879 and closed in 1952. In earlier years the station was widely used by travellers to Leicester, Grantham, Melton

Scalford church, dedicated to St Egelwin who is thought to be buried in the churchyard

Mowbray and Nottingham. Farmers sent their milk by train, cattle and horses were loaded and unloaded in the sidings and the station, with the adjoining coal yard, was busy and prosperous. This former station and goods yard is now a small industrial estate.

William Brown, a Scalford man, known as 'Peppermint Billy', was the last person to be executed in public at Leicester Prison in 1856. He was found guilty of murdering Edward and James Woodcock at Thorpe Toll Bar, having earlier been transported for ten years to Tasmania for stealing silver spoons at Newtown Linford.

The largest house in the parish, Scalford Hall, once the home of Colonel Colman (of mustard fame) was built in 1908 and is now used as a conference centre and the stables as a nursing home.

Of special interest in Scalford is the old market cross in the churchyard and the recently restored wash dyke on the Station Road.

Scraptoft

The original hamlet, population 60, consisted of Manor Farm and cottages on Scraptoft Rise; the Hall, with its dower house, Nether Hall, built in 1709; cottages in Main Street; the vicarage and the church, which dates back to the 12th century. At the beginning of the 20th century there was a blacksmith's, which has now gone. The former Pear Tree Inn, dated 1703, is now a newsagent's. Adjoining this is a fruiterer's, a Co-op store, a garage and a hairdresser's, which cater well for the needs of a growing population living in houses built after the Second World War. Some old cottages still remain in Main Street.

On the east side of the village, on the highest point, is the church. This adjoins Scraptoft Hall, which is a Queen Anne mansion standing in its own grounds, overlooking a small lake and framed by a background of trees.

In 1954 the Hall and extensive grounds were sold to Leicester Education Committee, who converted it into a teachers training college. The very attractive front was left untouched, all the building extensions taking place at the rear. Eventually the Leicester Polytechnic took it over and it is now known as the 'Scraptoft Campus'.

To the south of the village is an imposing building known as The White House. This was built by Mr Crumbie, who, when Normanton Hall in Rutland was demolished about 1926, bought the stones, together with additional ones from Derbyshire. The stones were all numbered and transported to Scraptoft, where they lay on the site for a considerable time. When the house was eventually built, Mr Crumbie only enjoyed living in it for a month when he died. For many years the house was occupied by the Harrison family, who took a keen interest in all aspects of village life. Mr Harrison was a seed merchant and the business eventually became known as Asmer Seeds. The White House is now owned by a brewery company and is the only public house in the village.

Another well known resident was the late Mr A. T. Sharpe, who for many years lived at Nether Hall. The nearby Leicester Council estate is known as Nether Hall Estate, as part of it was built on Mr Sharpe's land. Mr Sharpe owned many cottages and farms in the district and took a keen interest in the village. He was churchwarden for many years and a trustee of the village hall. In the earlier part of this century he was Captain of Leicestershire Cricket Club, being a gentleman player (the gentlemen were all amateurs). Mr Sharpe started the Scraptoft cricket club and their pitch was on one of his fields.

Adjacent to the village hall is a complex of nine houses and four bungalows, surrounded by large lawns. These are the Leicester and Leicestershire War Memorial Foundation Homes, which were opened in 1957 and are occupied by ex-servicemen and their families.

Seaton 🐚

Seaton, Rutland, is a small village nestling on the south facing slope of the Welland valley. The settlement has had a long history, evidenced by Roman and Saxon remains found in recent times.

The church, All Hallows, dates from Norman times, and the original chancel arch and doorway still exist. The building was added to in the mid-14th century and substantially renovated in the late 19th century.

The manors of Seaton came under the common ownership of the Sheffield family in the 17th century, who built a large stone house as their Hall in the centre of the village. The manor house survives to this day. The manor later belonged to the Tryons of Bulwick and then the Moncktons of Fineshade.

Seaton became a major railway junction in the late 19th century. In 1882 the Welland valley viaduct was completed and spanned three quarters of a mile across the valley. It is still in use. Its construction of 82 arches needed 2,000 men to labour for four years so a temporary settlement near Seaton, called Cyprus, was built to house them.

The village itself was once much larger with many more cottages, which have since been demolished. The present population is about 200.

This is composed mainly of business commuters and retired people. There are three family farms which used to be major employers for village people. The railway and Corby steelworks were also main places of work.

Seaton provided many other services including two butcher's shops, a bakery, carpenter and undertaker, a cobbler, blacksmith, general store and a maltings and brewhouse with two public houses. Only the post office and the George and Dragon pub survive today.

Village life used to be much more active. Not only did most people work within the village, but they lived as a community. The cricket team used to play regularly in the centre of the village and the pubs were more than mere watering holes with the lively domino and whist teams. The village celebrated Seaton Feast (first Sunday after 25th July) until the 1920s. Ploughboy Monday also lapsed at about the same time. The ploughboys would black their faces and dance round the village collecting for an ale party that evening.

The Royce family originated from Seaton where they were millers. One of their descendants became a partner of the world famous firm, Rolls-Royce.

Many of the older Seaton residents remember travelling to school on the 'Push and Pull'. This small train of two carriages travelled the lines from Seaton to Uppingham or Seaton to Stamford but was made redundant in 1966 when Seaton station closed.

Shangton

Shangton is a small village and always has been. At present there are eight households with a population of 21.

The name is derived from the Old English 'Scanca' meaning a shank or leg. This is because it lies at the foot of a spur formed by two streams which flow into a tributary of the Welland.

The church is 11th century and has ancient grave slabs within as well as in the churchyard. The old rectory is now known as The Manor House. The present rector lives at Gaulby, one of the seven parishes of the benefice.

The oldest house is 'Hall Farm', formerly known as 'The Old Hall'. In the garden is an impressive 17th century stone archway which was the gateway of the original entrance. The garden also has a magnificent walnut tree which must be several hundred years old.

There appears to be no record of unusual customs, myths or legends, but from a few old prints of the village it can be seen to have been a beautiful place. It was approached by an avenue of ancient wych elms but sadly these were lost through Dutch elm disease. However, Shangton is still a peaceful backwater surrounded mainly by pasture land.

Sharnford 🐚

Sharnford, with its population of around 1,000, stands two miles from the Warwickshire border, straddling the B4114.

The name is believed to derive from the Anglo-Saxon 'scarn', a division, which is very apt as, until the building of a foot and horse bridge in 1780, the two halves of the village were very much divided by a ford. In these modern times a 'proper' bridge carries a large amount of traffic between Leicester and Coventry.

On the parish boundary stands the Highcross Monument, which marks the crossing of the Roman Watling and Fosse roads. Part of the Fosse, long since forgotten by vehicular traffic, has recently been made more accessible to pedestrians and several adjacent fields have been environmentally improved to form 'Fosse Meadows'. Given time for the ponds to attract inhabitants and the trees to grow, this should one day be an attractive and interesting nature area.

The Evergreen Hall is the centre for most village activities. The 12th century parish church, dedicated to St Helen, was badly damaged by fire in 1984 but was soon lovingly restored. The Methodist chapel, built in 1827, is the oldest chapel still used for worship in the Hinckley Methodist Circuit. A good relationship exists between the two congregations. This was not always the case, as in December 1851 some dispute arose with the rector concerning the burial of one Joseph Clarke, aged 18 years. As a result he was buried in the chapel forecourt and the following year his family donated a piece of land as a burial ground at the rear of the building.

Shearsby 🐚

Shearsby is a small village of Saxon origin (Cherisbye) with about 200 inhabitants. The village lies in a valley nine miles south of Leicester. The houses, which vary from Tudor timber to modern brick, are mainly arranged round the village green, overlooked by the church built high on a mound and easily visible from many parts of the village. The last shop closed with the arrival of city supermarkets, but two thriving public houses remain.

About 140 years ago the population was twice the size it is now, with most people employed within the village. There were nine farmers, with butchers, bakers, a tallow chandler and a miller making the village self-sufficient. The village now has four farmers with only a few of the village inhabitants working locally, such as builders and hoteliers.

In the early part of the 1800s Shearsby was known for its famous salt spring. The spring was to be found one half mile to the south of the village, near the Bruntingthorpe Road. It formed a round pit ten or twelve yards in circumference and about one and a half yards deep when full. The water tasted salty and brackish and it was said that no cattle would drink from the spring. However, one villager who suffered from scurvy found great benefit from drinking and bathing in the spring. It was thought at the time that if the spring were recommended by a few doctors it might become popular and equal any Royal spa in the country. Now the Bath Hotel is the only reminder of the efficacious spring, water from which was supplied to special baths in the cellar of the hotel where patrons could 'take the waters'.

It is a steep climb up to the church, which is dedicated to St Mary Magdalen. In the churchyard, the earliest legible gravestone is of an Anglican priest who died on 11th April 1601. One of the upright stones is – 'In memory of William Weston who was unfortunately catched in the windmill, and expired April 8th 1756 aged 36'.

The main road travelling south climbs steeply as it passes by Shearsby, overhung by trees with two coverts either side. Many years ago a brother and a sister lived close by. Their names were John and Jane Ball. It was said that when coaches travelling to Northampton slowed down to climb the hill, John and Jane would appear from behind the trees with pistols cocked, to hold up and rob the unwary travellers. Eventually John and Jane were caught and hanged on either side of the road. The coverts are now known by the names of John Ball and Jane Ball.

Shepshed 🪶

Shepshed was at one point in its history a centre for the stockinger trade and was then larger than Loughborough, the nearest large town now. Knitwear and sock making are still a large industry here.

Thirty years ago it was still possible to hear the older generation talking in a local dialect which was indecipherable to incomers.

152

Not much of the original village remains and large parts of the surrounding countryside have been built over. Where once badgers lived there is now a large housing estate.

Originally Shepshed had a railway and was going to have a canal, but this was never completed and the cut has now been built on, the only remaining part being the aqueduct.

There are follies in the park of Garendon Hall but only a lodge remains where the Hall once stood. Also in the gardens are graves of monks whose abbey once stood here. In the drystone wall surrounding the grounds can be seen some of the original abbey stonework.

Sibson, Upton & Wellsborough

'Sibetesdone' was first mentioned in the Domesday Book of 1086, with approximately 700 acres held by Earl Aubrey de Couci. The village has had through the centuries such names as 'Sybbedesdoune' and is now Sibson.

The church and the Cock Inn are the most dominant features in Sibson. St Botolph's parish church is very picturesque from all angles. The date of foundation is uncertain but there is evidence of a church on the site in 1154 and a record of rectors from 1201. The Feast Day, 17th June, was at one time celebrated by a fair or 'Wake'.

The tower contains four bells; one of which has the inscription:

> 'All you that hear my mournefull sound,
> Repent before your layd in ground'!

The Cock Inn was built in 1250 and, being over 700 years old, is known as one of the loveliest inns in the country. One famous 'gentleman' to visit it is said to have been the notorious highwayman Dick Turpin in 1735. Until 1935 this inn belonged to the Church and it was closed on Sundays until 1954. During the Second World War the inn sign was stolen, believed to have been taken back to America by the visiting forces!

Wellsborough is steeped in history. Folklore says the earlier Temple Hall derived from the Knights Templar. Today Temple Hall Farm is built near the old site.

A convalescent home for printers was built here in 1920 but during the Second World War it became the headquarters for the Labour Party.

There are early records of chapels at both Wellsborough and Upton,

153

but there is no record of the chapel at Wellsborough after the 14th century.

Upton has few claims to fame. It was first recorded in 1196 and was totally agricultural. There was a Baptist church in Main Street which has now gone and a house stands in its place. The boundary of Upton is a Roman road, now known as Fenn Lane.

At the Atherstone Fair, in days not so long ago, Upton was famous for its Leicestershire cheese!

In the 18th and 19th centuries, the Chapmans of Upton Lodge Farm kept Longhorn cattle. A pair of these horns are preserved in the village hall, Sibson. Robert Bakewell's famous bull *Tuppeny* sired the Upton herd and many prizes were won at Royal Shows.

The land today in Sibson and District is still agricultural and very rural.

Skeffington 🐑

If you drive east along the A47 from Leicester, at the end of the Billesdon bypass you will enter the parish of Skeffington. On your right, standing in parkland well back from the road, is Skeffington Hall, and the village lies to the east and south of it. There has been a settlement here since before the Norman Conquest, and for much of its history the village has been owned, and the villagers employed, by the occupants of the Hall.

Today Skeffington is very much a commuter village. Many professions and skills are represented here, but few people are employed within the parish. There is some work on the land, and there is an animal feed mill within the boundary, but otherwise the only employment offered is at the local pub/restaurant or with horses.

There are around 50 houses within the village and another 20 or so in the parish, isolated farms and cottages; the Hall dates from Tudor times and there are some lovely old cottages, some thatched, also remaining. These together with a number of 'estate' houses built in Victorian times make up half the village, the rest of the houses having been built since the 1950s. The village inn, the Fox & Hounds, once had quite a parcel of land attached to it. It was probably a drover's inn – a stopping off place for herdsmen in bygone days taking sheep and cattle to market.

The heavy clay soils of this part of Leicestershire make fine pasture and early settlers would have reared sheep – the name of the village is derived from the Saxon word 'sceaft' meaning sheep. Sheep rearing still represents an important part of farming in these parts.

Skeffington has long standing connections with the fox hunting world and one of its rectors, Reverend Davenport, was a famous hunting parson. At one time an offshoot of the Quorn Hunt, which later became the Fernie Hunt, was based here and there is still a Kennel Cottage where the hounds used to be housed. Sir Richard Sutton and Mr W. Tailby, who both owned the Hall during Victorian times, were involved with the Hunt and were responsible for the building of housing for estate and hunt servants at this time. Sir Richard also spent a great deal of money on restoring the church, dedicated to St Thomas Becket. Very little of its 12th century origins are now visible, although some impressive monuments to the Skeffingtons are still to be seen.

Skeffington lacks a village hall but is not lacking in community spirit. All interests join together to stage fetes and dances and other social events on premises kindly made available by village residents. Meeting places are the church, the 'local' and the village post office/general store.

Slawston

Slawston lies in the south-east corner of Leicestershire. The village predates the Norman Conquest and was mentioned as 'Slagestone' or 'Slachestone' during the reign of William the Conqueror.

The Boyville family obtained the manor in the 15th century. After John Boyville died in 1468 the manor was purchased by the Brudenell family of Stonton Wyville. Today, over five centuries later, Brudenells still own land at Slawston and Othorpe.

Othorpe is now a lost village and only one house stands on the site. Little is known of its fate but in 1258, five tenants held three parcels of land there and the village may have become depopulated in the late 14th or 15th century. This could have been associated with the conversion from arable land to pasture, as it became important sheep pasture under the Brudenells.

Under the Brudenells, at the end of the 17th century, the manorial court for Slawston, Stonton Wyville, Glooston and Cranoe was held at Slawston, so obviously this village was the most important on the estate.

Behind Slawston church is a hill which at one time housed a windmill. This was built in 1637 and a replica remained there until 1928 when unfortunately it was burnt down. No insurance had been taken out on the building so it was never rebuilt. But some older inhabitants still remember the mill and its disastrous fate.

The church of All Saints is built of ironstone and limestone and dates from the late 13th century. Substantial repairs were carried out in the early 14th century and again in 1864 a thorough restoration took place.

The Rev Thomas Hope in his will in 1769 left £100 in trust for the village, the annual interest to be expended on coal for eight of the poorest inhabitants, of whom the parish clerk was always to be one. Anyone convicted of stealing fuel or breaking hedges was to be excluded! In 1786 the parish received an anonymous gift of £12.7s. These sums were invested and the interest distributed in coal to the poor, the clerk always receiving one-eighth of the whole. These days, the annual interest would buy very little and certainly not bags of coal for eight people!

At one time the village had two pubs, the Black Horse and the Blue Lion, plus a shop and a post office. Now these amenities have gone and, to the casual visitor, Slawston is a quiet unassuming place. However, if you look beneath the surface you will find friendly people who all pull together to keep the heart of this small community alive.

Smeeton Westerby 🌿

Smeeton Westerby is a small village in the middle of Fernie Hunt country, lying about nine miles south east of Leicester and less than a mile from its neighbour, Kibworth. Although Smeeton Westerby is lucky enough to share many of Kibworth's facilities, most of its villagers prefer to remain independent.

The village was once two separate hamlets, Smeeton and Westerby, and the boundary between the two is said to be marked by two white stones adjacent to Westerby House.

Farming was, until recently, one of the few sources of income in Smeeton. During the 19th century, framework knitting was important locally. Because of their large top-floor windows, the terraced houses on Pit Hill were said to have housed some of the knitters.

In 1936, a brick building north east of the church was sold by a hosiery manufacturer to J. E. Slater of Kibworth who designed and made display materials. This was an important source of employment in the village for about 40 years.

Smeeton Westerby is a conservation village so there has been little change in its size or lay-out over the last 50 years. The former factory site and a small development on Mill Lane make up most of the new houses and the village consists chiefly of a mixture of buildings along the winding main street.

The houses range from old cottages and farmhouses to more modern council houses built this century. The old forge building still stands on the corner of Main Street and Blacksmith's Lane and has been converted, along with four small cottages, to one large cottage. Westerby House is a large 18th century brick built house facing the south end of the main street. This was occupied by the rector of Kibworth in the second half of the 19th century.

Along the main street is an interesting ironstone wall which still retains the mullioned windows of the former house. This was saved from being demolished largely by the efforts of Smeeton residents who considered that it added to the character of the village.

An ancient burial ground of the Beaker people was found in 1975 just outside Smeeton. One of the new roads in the village is named after the site.

Somerby 🐖

Somerby is a mixed stone and brick village with the houses right alongside a typical dog-legged Leicestershire High Street.

Turn into High Street from the Melton/Oakham road and, in a hollow on the right, is the horse pond. It is said to be exceptionally deep. There is even a legend that a coachman once backed his coach in to allow the horses to drink and it sank, complete with passengers!

Next comes the fine church. Unusually, its bell tower lies between the chancel and the nave. There is a memorial window to the 10th Battalion of the Parachute Regiment, many of whose members were billeted in the village before embarking for Arnhem. The final briefing was given in the old Memorial Institute, which has since been demolished. In the entrance to the new hall (next to the Stilton Cheese Inn) there is a memorial to the Somerby war dead and to the Arnhem parachutists. Every September on the Sunday nearest to the anniversay of Arnhem, there is a parade and reunion of the gradually diminishing group of veterans.

In the churchyard is the grave of Somerby-born Dr Benjamin Richardson who became one of the most famous surgeons in early Victorian London. He was famous not for skill or science but for speed – by far the most important aspect of surgery practised without anaesthesia.

On the High Street, past the shops, is Somerby Garage which started life as a manufacturer of bicycles. Next door is the late-Victorian stone school. Opposite is a group of brick houses which was formerly a dame school. Behind the house called 'The Old Forge' was the Somerby Electric

157

Light Company which supplied the better-off residents until 1933 when the National Grid took over.

Somerby is still a thriving community. It has, besides church and chapel, a school, shops, garage, surgery, pubs, a building firm and a bus company.

Before the First World War the main activity next to farming was the Hunt. Some of the houses on the High Street and side streets were hunting boxes where many local people worked as domestic servants and grooms. Now, with the closure of Grove Stud, all that has ended. Nowadays many people who hunt come just for the day. Grove Stud, on the final bend of the village, is at present being converted into retirement homes.

South Kilworth ✎

South Kilworth stands on the southern border of Leicestershire. The present population of 400 has remained steady over the years. It is situated on crossroads and in the past supported five alehouses – a suitable stopping-off place for the drovers urging their animals to the nearby market towns. Today there is one public house (The White Hart), a post office cum general store, a butcher, a primary school, a Congregational church and the parish church dedicated to St Nicholas.

In a niche over the church porch can be seen the statue of St Nicholas. Legend has it that after the battle of Naseby in 1645 Oliver Cromwell rode through the village and, catching sight of the statue, demanded to know why it had not been sent crashing down with the rest of the Catholic images. 'It's only old Nick, so we left him', was the reply from a quick-thinking trooper.

Between 1817 and 1847 Dr William Pearson was rector of the parish. He was a co-founder and treasurer of the Royal Astronomical Society and famous for many books on practical astronomy. He purchased the instrument that became known as the South Kilworth Altitude and Azimuth Circle when Napoleon's invasion of Russia prevented it going to the observatory in St Petersburg. He erected a large rotative astronomical dome over a wing of the rectory and in 1834 built an observatory off the Rugby Road, which is now used as a private house.

At the Harvest Thanksgiving service in 1856 villagers were called from the church to save their homes. A fire had started at Mr 'Baker' Hill's premises, putting at risk at least half of the thatched houses. The fire was duly extinguished and the service resumed the following evening.

In recent years new industries have come to the village. There is a flourishing agricultural engineering business, a nursery supplying alpines and dwarf conifers to the horticultural trade and a Soil Association approved organic smallholding. Half an acre of this produces Muller Thurgau grapes for commercial wine making, while the remaining land is used to grow fruit and vegetables. Several village families are engaged in farming, though most wage-earners are now commuters to nearby towns.

South Luffenham

The clear flowing stream, a tributary of the Chater, first brought Anglo Saxon settlers to the village. In the 19th century the water was backed up to provide power to the watermill, and the stream partially silted up. Until the 1940s, when it closed, the watermill was used for the grinding of feed grains. The windmill stood on the opposite bank, close to the watermill. This lost its top in a great storm in 1895 and has not worked since. Today a plastics factory and a number of small businesses occupy the site.

Running almost parallel to the stream is the track of the old railway, closed in the 1960s. Not only has the physical shape of the village been affected by the railway, but many of the thatched houses and barns in the village were lost indirectly through it. On the 19th April, 1913 the 2 pm 'football special' to Market Harborough was getting up steam to get up the hill. The strong wind carried sparks to a 'goss n'faggit hovel' in Pridmore's yard. The fire spread quickly and the thatch of the houses and barns in the square were soon destroyed.

Perhaps the most elegant house in the village is the Hall, built in the late 17th century of local stone. Today the gardens are well known both for their beauty and their botanic interest. The annual open day, for the benefit of St Mary's church, draws visitors from far around.

The increasing mechanisation of agriculture has done much to change the nature of the village. In 1846 the majority of the population of 317 were engaged in farming the 1,440 acres of the parish, the only other recorded trades being a butcher, a grocer and two publicans. There are still two public houses in the village. The Boot and Shoe was so-called for the nearby premises of a shoemaker. There are villagers who clearly remember the premises also being used as the village bakehouse, where a Sunday dinner could be cooked for twopence. The Halfway House is so-called as it was the halfway coaching house between Uppingham and Stamford.

Next to the Boot and Shoe is the church, dedicated to St Mary the Virgin, and begun soon after the Norman Conquest. At the entrance to the vestry is a memorial to Rose Boswell, daughter of one king of the gipsies, who died in 1793 while her family were encamped at nearby Fosters Bridge. The churchwardens originally refused her burial, as she was not a Christian, but the curate overruled them. The slab was paid for by collections from many gipsies as a mark of respect to their king.

The church also contains a 14th century effigy of a member of the Culpepper family. It was the custom to place a sickle on the neck of the effigy on the last Sunday in August, and other feast Sundays. The village feast was held on the first Sunday after the 15th August, on the Bell-ringers' field. This is so called after the bells of South Luffenham church guided an elderly woman across the foggy common from Tixover. In gratitude she donated a field whose income should pay the sexton to ring the bells at 5 am and 8 pm daily from the end of October to the 25th March. This continued until the outbreak of the First World War.

The most internationally notorious former resident was a pupil at the school held in the rectory by the Rev Richards at the beginning of the century; Hermann Goering, Hitler's second in command. It is popularly believed that he carved his initials on one of the window frames and that during the Second World War he gave specific instructions that the Stamford area was not to be bombed, as he intended to make nearby Burghley House his residence after the invasion. Although the village has seen many radical changes over the centuries, at least it was spared that!

Sproxton

Sproxton is a village of some 70 houses, with a population of about 170. The village has many old farmhouses built of orange brown marlstone, and cottages built of the same stone or a deep red coloured brick.

Sproxton has a very old church, about 700 years old, with a large square Norman tower. It is about a quarter of a mile from the present village, though the site of the old medieval manor house can be seen in the field next to the church, together with the remains of three ancient fish ponds. In the churchyard is one of only a few complete Saxon crosses now remaining in the country. This cross has had an interesting history. When Nicholls wrote his county history in 1795 it was being used as a footbridge on a path to Saltby and only the base was left in the churchyard. Nicholls says that it had not been removed within the memory of the oldest inhabitant in the village, and that the upper side had worn quite smooth from the passage of many feet. It was rescued sometime during the 19th century and replaced in the churchyard – where one side is indeed smooth, but the other three sides intricately carved.

The church used to have only three bells, very interesting medieval ones, but unringable. However, in 1985 a peal of eight bells was installed from a redundant church in Leicester, All Saints. The bells were taken to the church in the time honoured way on a farm wagon, with the tenor decorated, and many of the villagers following. Ringers from the village now ring the bells for services in the church.

Sproxton has been a farming village for generations. Around 1850 there were 16 farmers and seven cottagers, and of a total population of 427, 63 men were employed as agricultural workers. By the 1930s only eight farmers and six smallholders were left, and today there are only two farms in the village, and as few as six men working on the land. In the 19th century Sproxton was virtually self-sufficient, with millers, wheelwrights, a mason, shoemakers, blacksmiths, and even a straw bonnet maker. The village also had three tailors, two drapers, a butcher, baker and grocer, two pubs and an alehouse.

Around the turn of the century, from the 1890s to the 1940s, ironstone was mined on Saltby Heath adjoining the village, and many men from the village worked at the mines. The work was hard, but the hours shorter and the pay better than in farming, and a close-knit community grew up in the village. Today many people from the village work in varied jobs in Melton Mowbray and Grantham, both about ten miles away. Two haulage firms and a garden furniture business operate from the village, and there are still two shops, one of which includes the post office, and a pub.

The original village school was erected in 1800 by the Duke of Rutland, then the major landowner in the village. It was replaced by the present Victorian Gothic building in 1871. The school has one room and was attended by as many as 100 children in the 1880s. In those days children stayed at Sproxton until they were old enough to leave school and begin work, mainly in the fields or in domestic service.

Various customs and fairs are associated with the village. Until the 1890s an annual hiring fair was held on the green on the day after Martinmas (12th November) when farm workers were hired for the coming year. The village feast was held until the 1840s on the second Sunday in September, when it was changed to Whit Sunday. Within living memory an annual fair was held on the green on Whit Monday, followed by a feast supper in the upper room at the pub.

Cricket has been played in the village for generations, the first match recorded in the Grantham Journal being against Skillington in 1856, the players repairing to the Crown Inn after the game. The village still has a thriving cricket club with a cricket pitch and pavilion.

Stapleton ❧

Stapleton lies on the turnpike, now known as the A447, between Hinckley and Market Bosworth. The earliest known reference to it is in a charter from the King of Mercia in AD 833.

The church of St Martin is thought to date from about 1300 and King Richard III is reputed to have spent the night of 21st August 1485 resting in the church before the battle of Bosworth Field.

There were two toll gates, two pubs, a blacksmith's shop and a wheelwright in the village. The wheelwright was a true craftsman, sawing his wood over a sawpit, making farm carts and wagons by hand. He could 'line his wheels' and do decorative freehand lettering on the carts. He also turned his hand to coffin making when required. The Mill House, which has a preservation order, is now a residence. Unfortunately nothing remains of the old mill where the wheelwright used to make the cogs from applewood, on which the mill turned.

The village school was built in 1848 but closed in the 1930s. It then became first the church room and later the village hall. Today, by public subscription, the village hall has been extended to accommodate twice the number of people.

The Methodist chapel was built in 1852 and rebuilt in 1905, enjoying a good congregation, flourishing Sunday school and Bible Class, with Mr Tom Harris as superintendent/caretaker for many years. Mr Robert Belcher followed him but was also the village roadman, renowned for the great care he lavished on keeping the grass verges cut and levelled 'just so'.

In the first half of the 20th century 18 houses were built but later a small estate increased the size of the village considerably. It used to have a regular bus service before car ownership became widespread. After the First World War, villagers moved from farming into the boot and shoe industry. Several large farms, which were labour intensive, were bought by the County Council and then split up into smallholdings of around 50 acres. Each holding employed few people, being fully mechanised.

Electricity came to the village in the 1940s but not to the outlying farms until 1949. There, paraffin lamps, candles and hurricane lamps were the order of the day.

Nowadays Stapleton village has become a commuter haven, with people travelling far and wide to work, but it still retains its agricultural flavour and heritage with the farms that remain.

Stoney Stanton

Originally called Stony Staunton, the village was mentioned in the Domesday Book (1086) as Stantone. Lying between the old Fosse Way and the river Soar, the village stands on a bed of basalt and granite rock. Several quarries produced setts and edging stones which were much used locally as well as farther afield. Closely connected with Sapcote, a certain amount of rivalry has always existed between the two villages. Three outlying areas of Stoney Stanton are Clint Hill, Lane's Hill and Mill Hill – the latter being famous for its fairy rings.

By 1811 the village contained 95 houses and early industry was mainly farming and small shopkeeping. Almost every cottage kitchen would have a 'Griswold' knitting frame and the hosiery would be collected by one woman and taken into the Hinckley factories. At one time three bakers, three butchers and two cobblers operated in the village.

Around 1860 quarrying began, employing many men from this area. There were blacksmiths, sett makers, kerb dressers and later engine drivers. Early morning and late evening the quarry horses could be heard trekking through the village. Before 1880 the Mountsorrel Granite Company acquired two quarries and began to modernise the stone extraction process. Buildings of note built of this fine granite and still standing are:- the Working Men's Club (originally a quarrymen's reading room), two schools, two large private houses and the south side of St Michael's church. A few granite street walls are still to be seen.

Three churches served the community. St Michael's parish church and the Methodist church are both still very much alive with regular services. The Congregational chapel is sadly now closed, but converted and used as the village Boy Scout headquarters. At St Michael's the first recorded curate was in 1185, though the church building is thought to be mainly 14th century. It has an impressive spire and a peal of eight bells. Worthy of note is the Norman tympanum over the outer vestry door.

Since the 1960s the village has grown considerably, with four large housing estates and more building planned. A large primary school was built and opened in April 1969, a community centre was added and later parents worked hard to provide funds to build a school swimming pool.

Stoney Cove, formerly Top Pit and Lane's Hill quarries, is now nationally known as a popular water sports centre. The complex is used for underwater diving, ski-ing and testing of MOD amphibious vehicles.

John Bold, former scholar and teacher, gained a Cambridge degree and gave Stoney Stanton 49 precious years of his life. He was a most famous curate at St Michael's, living on a stipend of £30 per annum! Ministering from 1702–1751 he led a frugal existence and was able to leave money in trust to the village. He is buried in the churchyard.

More recently, Nigel Lawson, MP for the Blaby constituency, has resided here in the Old Rectory for many years. He is at the moment Chancellor of the Exchequer.

Swinford

Swinford is a small attractive village which is situated close to the borders of both Warwickshire and Northamptonshire. The name Swinford is said to have derived from 'Swineford': the place where herds of swine were driven over the ford in the village stream.

Being one of a group of four parishes, Swinford has a church, All Saints, which dates from the 13th century and has been restored many times. The church has a Saxon font which is thought to be one of the oldest in England.

In the past Swinford was basically a farming community, although it could also boast many other trades within the village and many travelling traders would visit with their wares. A 'Saltmonger' came in a four wheeled covered wagon selling large blocks of salt about 18 × 24 inches, which were purchased to salt the pig meat. A 'Fishman' came with a pony and cart and the 'Pea Lady' would visit annually selling peas at one shilling per 8 lb bag. A hardware merchant and a rag and bone man also called.

Within the village there was a thriving blacksmith's forge, a butcher's shop and several bakeries – one of which also provided the service to villagers of roasting their joints or baking their rice puddings. Children scurrying back and forth with trays of covered dishes was a common sight. There was a post office which also housed the draper's, the rate assessor and the collector of taxes! The post was driven to Rugby by horse. The stables are still intact. The village manor house was converted to a grocer's shop over 100 years ago but in recent years it has been restored to a dwelling.

Today there is still a post office/general store in Swinford and a few small businesses operate from within the village. There are two public houses, one being the Cave Arms which is said to date back to 1650. It is a picturesque building with a thatched roof and it takes its name from the Cave family who have lived at nearby Stanford Hall for centuries. In the past the 'Cave' doubled as a doctor's surgery every Tuesday at 11 am sharp! The other public house is the Chequers, where it is said a local character, Mr Penny, used to arrive each evening with his pony and trap on which was placed his large harp and his small dog. He would entertain his eager audience whilst his dog sat beside him drinking beer.

Swinford has had some connections with famous historical characters, including Katherine de Swynford, who was born in 1350. She was the wife of local inhabitant Hugh de Swynford and after his death she married John of Gaunt. Their granddaughter was Margaret Beaufort, mother of Henry VII.

Disaster has played a part in the history of Swinford. In 1740 the 'Great Fire of Swinford' devastated 15 houses. Barns, stables, outhouses, goods, animal feed, fuel and livestock were also lost. The cost of the damage was estimated to be £2,500, a considerable amount in those days.

Theddingworth 🐝

The small village of Theddingworth, with a population of about 160, is on the busy main road from Market Harborough to Lutterworth. Originally called 'Dedigworde' in the Domesday Book, the medieval village was on a site to the north of the village church. Traces of the medieval village still remain and the area is listed as a site of special scientific interest. There is also evidence of an Iron Age fort.

Theddingworth houses are mainly of red brick and slate with a few notable exceptions. 'Pebble Cottages' on the Sibbertoft Road, built in 1829, are a block of six back-to-back three-storeyed cottages. The walls are pebbles or 'duckies' with brick dressings. The entire top storey, at one time, housed an industry making silk plush for top hats, with workers living on the first and second storeys.

The pretty thatched house on the Station Road was formerly a butcher's shop, probably of 17th century origin.

Hothorpe Hall, just across the county boundary, now a religious conference centre, was the residence of the lords of the manor of Theddingworth. In 1831 the 2nd Earl Spencer was the lord of the manor.

In the middle of Theddingworth the roads run north-west to Mowsley and south-east to Sibbertoft. The Sibbertoft Road, constructed in

1830 to replace the old road to Hothorpe, crosses the river Welland 200 yards from the village. This is the boundary with Northamptonshire.

The Grand Union Canal runs through the north of the parish and was opened in 1814. It is now used extensively for pleasure barges and angling; the towpath makes a picturesque walk.

The church of All Saints, built in the 13th century of ironstone and limestone, is in the centre of the village. It is now in a group of four parishes and the vicar lives out of the village. There are many interesting features in the church; a Snetzler organ dating from 1754 is one of only three in the country.

John Smeeton, who lived at Beeches Farm, built the Smeeton Institute as a reading room and billiard room in 1893 in memory of his son. This building was extended for the Queen's Silver Jubilee in 1977 and is used as the village hall.

The Congregational chapel, of red brick, was built in 1833 and stands adjacent to the village hall. The chapel had its own school from 1870 to 1880 when it amalgamated with the main village school.

Agriculture has always been the main industry in the village and remains so today. However, the majority of the people work outside the village, some even commuting to London.

Once a year money is distributed to the elderly in the village by virtue of an ancient charity, 'The Poor's Land'. The money is provided by the rent from a field on the Bosworth Road.

Thornton

The small village of Thornton with its 1,300 inhabitants lies to the north-west of Leicester.

It was a 'township' as far back as 1086. The name was derived from 'Town of Thorns', even today they still grow in great abundance, much to the discomfort of the canine population. With its reservoir and surrounding woods, magnificent trees and quiet peaceful atmosphere it is a well known beauty spot.

The reservoir was made in 1853 and water from it was the first to be piped into Leicester to the Temperance Hall. Tall Scots Pine and Larch trees line the pleasant walk around the stretch of water which is now used for pleasure only, namely fishing and sailing.

One of the oldest cottages was built as an inn at the turnpike. The plaque on the wall bears the date 1666, the same date as the great fire of London. It is now called Mere Cottage but as an inn it was called 'The

Stork'. The large cellar that runs the length of the cottage kept the ale at the correct temperature. A village water pump was situated at the turnpike. The supply never dried up and it was a meeting place for villagers to pass the time of day. A housing estate was built in 1949/50 when the population was 786. This rose to 984 in 1981.

Thornton church dates back to 1189 and has many interersting features. An inner door which is reputed to have come from Ulverscroft Priory has medieval metal work of 12th or 13th century make. Beside the door handle there is a 'sanctuary ring'. Legend has it that a criminal fleeing from justice would lay hold of the ring and would be safe for a certain time.

Early in the 1950s the village blacksmith still lived in the middle of the Main Street. There were two grocery shops, a chapel and a large building that was a men's meeting house. This building no longer exists. There were ten farms in those days, now only five are used as such.

Thrussington 🐑

Thrussington is situated in the valley of the river Wreake. Travelling from the nearby village of Rearsby, a pleasant view of the old ironstone church across the river Wreake welcomes the visitor to this small village, giving an impression of peace and tranquillity.

The majority of the houses and buildings in this attractive village are situated in the southern end of the parish. The green is sited in the centre of the village and is surrounded by houses, three shops and, on the north-west side, the Star Inn, which has the date 1744 on its walls.

The church, dedicated to the Holy Trinity, is the oldest building in the village. It has seen many changes over the centuries, both inside and out. Inside, it has 13th century arcades, late 14th century clerestory lights, and on the west end wall of the church are the marks of three different roofs.

The oldest house, now called Bridgland House and once known as Bridge Farm, dates from the 15th century. It is a cruck type cottage, timber with brick infilling. No doubt originally it would have had a thatched roof. It stands on the corner of Hoby Road. Among the many farmhouses in the parish, the Manor and the Grange are medieval in origin.

The Thrussington Church of England primary school is situated in Hoby Road. As long ago as 1652 an amount of £6 per annum was settled on Thrussington school by Thomas Hayne, born here in 1582. *White's Directory of Leicestershire* (1846) mentions that the free school was rebuilt in 1837 by the trustees of the late Rev C. B. Woolley.

John Ferneley, famous for his paintings, mainly of horses and hunting scenes, was born in Thrussington in 1782. He was the son of a wheelwright, and until the age of 21 was apprenticed to his father's trade. In his spare time he painted pictures on the carts his father made. Encouraged by the Duke of Rutland, he eventually became a pupil of Ben Marshall, the famous portrait painter. He lived most of his life in Melton Mowbray, and died there on 3rd June, 1860. He is buried in Thrussington churchyard with his first wife and son, Claude Loraine. Thrussington is justly proud of John Ferneley, whose paintings are world famous and now sell for hundreds of thousands of pounds.

Thurcaston 🐛

Thurcaston, spelt 'Thurkiteleston' in the Domesday Book, was, at that time, part of a small lordship, and lay along what is now Mill Road and Anstey Lane, roughly parellel with the Rothley brook.

It is here, where Leicester Road forms the crossroad, that the old and new Thurcaston meet. On one corner of Mill Road stands the Wheatsheaf, a 400 year old coaching inn; thatched until 1929, and still a popular meeting place for travellers and locals alike. The Wright family held the unbroken tenancy for 105 years, and still live in the village, though no longer in the inn.

Farther along Mill Road from the inn is the Methodist chapel. In 1825 a cottage was purchased for £25, and was converted to become the smallest chapel in the county, seating just 30 worshippers.

A few yards along is Mill Farm. Once a thriving mill, it ceased operating after a fire destroyed the machinery, became a farm for some years, and is now a private residence. Beyond the traces of the mill race is the arboretum, planted in 1983, the trees donated by local people and societies.

The King William public house is also on Mill Road, the modern building replacing a cottage-type hostelry in the 1950s and within listening distance of the steam trains, on what was part of the Great Central Railway.

Across the road from the Wheatsheaf, on the corner of Anstey Lane, a new development of retirement bungalows is being built, recreating the old idea of living close together in a small community.

168

Between Leicester Road and the church on Anstey Lane is where the 'working' part of the village was situated. The farms are now dwelling houses and only traces of a bygone life are visible, such as the pump at the side of a pond in the forecourt of Thurcaston House, marking the farmhouse site.

Across the road is 'Latimer House', a cruck-framed thatched house, wrongly quoted in various histories as the birthplace of Bishop Hugh Latimer, the martyr. True, it was named after him, but it was a farmhouse whose exact age is not known. It was extended to an L shaped building during the reign of Elizabeth I. The attached smithy was still in use many years after the house was restored in 1936 by Miss Marjorie Sedgwick with her brother and sister.

The church of All Saints is also very old and shows considerable traces of early work incorporated in alterations and restorations from the 15th to 19th centuries. The Norman south doorway is the oldest part of the church, which was rebuilt in the 13th century. Here is a marble memorial to Bishop Latimer, Thurcaston's most famous son. He was born in a yeoman's house near the church in 1485, and martyred in Oxford in 1555. No trace of his home can be found, though it was probably underneath the stackyard of the present farm. There are old gravestones in the beautifully kept churchyard, dating from the early 17th century.

In the 1930s Thurcaston grew rapidly, the fashion for ribbon development lining the road from Leicester. Then ponds were drained and built over and farmland sold and developed. What was a small village of farms and workers in the nearby waterworks at Cropston, is now a village where every livelihood is represented.

Thurlaston

Thurlaston is a small village of some 600 souls. It could be said to be a typical English village, as it has a post office and general store, a Church Aided school, a church, a chapel and two public houses – one adjacent to the church, dating back to 1631 and the other next door to the chapel!

In the 19th and early 20th century, Thurlaston was a very compact village and self contained, having all the trades necessary to life. Everyone knew everyone, and many families were related. However, in the past 25 years or so, small new estates have been built.

Being a rural village, one would have thought that all the workers were connected with agriculture, but this was not so. In a lot of the older cottages (now demolished) hooks were found in the ceilings, denoting the presence of hand looms at some time. Obviously a proportion of the population was connected with the textile trade, possibly as outworkers. In fact before and during the Second World War Thurlaston boasted a small factory (now two cottages) for the making of hosiery, employing about 15 to 20 girls.

Thurlaston from the earliest times has always had a place of worship, and the present parish church was built in the 12th century. There have been sundry alterations, although the structure still remains Norman. A portion of this parish is called Normanton Turville after the family who resided in the manor there in Norman times. There are monuments in the church to the Turville family, the last of whom died in 1776.

Another area of Thurlaston which contained a moated manor at the time of Richard II is New Hall Park. At the present time there is a farmhouse on the site, and the surrounding farm is still known as New Hall Park just as the small area where the Turvilles lived, is still known as Normanton.

It is also interesting to note that there is a Dicks Hill in Thurlaston, supposedly part of the route taken by Richard III in 1485 on his way to Bosworth Field, where he was slain.

On the village boundary there is a ford across the road known as Watery Gate. Of course it draws children like a magnet! Water was not piped to the village until 1953, and sewerage pipes were not laid until 1956. Electricity was also not known here until the 1950s.

A Georgian house in the village known as the Holt was built as the rector's house in 1845 and remained the rector's house for many years. In the early part of this century poor people of the village could go to the kitchen there and obtain a bowl of soup. During the Second World War the house was inhabited by the nuns of the order of Perpetual Adoration; a Roman Catholic order whose London home had been bombed. In fact the bell to call them to prayer still remains on the roof of the Holt.

Thurnby, Bushby & Stoughton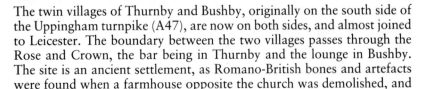

The twin villages of Thurnby and Bushby, originally on the south side of the Uppingham turnpike (A47), are now on both sides, and almost joined to Leicester. The boundary between the two villages passes through the Rose and Crown, the bar being in Thurnby and the lounge in Bushby. The site is an ancient settlement, as Romano-British bones and artefacts were found when a farmhouse opposite the church was demolished, and

Saxon tombstones were unearthed when the church was largely rebuilt in 1870–73.

The church of St Luke, in Thurnby, which serves both villages, is first mentioned in 1143 and shares its vicar with Stoughton. It has a square tower supported by four massive Norman pillars between the nave and chancel. Beautifully carved angels in the roof, and a communion table made by a local craftsman complement the east window, with its many lovely blues. This window was given by Mr J. A. Jackson, who had previously built Thurnby Court, reputedly with the profits of blockade-running in the American Civil War – he was a Liverpool cotton mer-

Thurnby Court before its demolition early this century

chant. This magnificent house had its own swimming pool, winter garden, stables and even gasworks, but a very short life, only from 1870 to 1916. Then it was demolished with the aid of dynamite and many windows in the village suffered that day.

There is a peal of eight bells in the tower of St Luke's, the oldest dated 1631. Thurnby remembers the Battle of the Bells, which took place in 1862. The bells were to be rung when the Quorn Hunt met in the village but the vicar objected and barred the door of the belfry. However, the parish constable prised open the door, the bells were rung for two hours

171

by the ringing band, one of whom was the churchwarden, and the vicar took the ringers to court. The Ecclesiastical Court of Arches decided in favour of the vicar but the four ringers refused to pay the fine imposed and were sent to prison for a month. Tradition says they lived like kings, being provided with many delicacies by the members of the Hunt.

There are few old houses in Thurnby and Bushby. The manor house dates back at least to the early 1600s, there are farmhouses which may be nearly as old and some very early cottages on Main Street, including Gilstead, which is thatched. The name of Charity Farm, at the east end of Bushby, records the gift of Richard Nedd, a London scrivener, to his birthplace of Mountsorrel. He willed £300 in trust to the mayor, bailiffs and burgesses of Leicester, to buy a piece of land with a rental value of £15 per annum, the money to be distributed to the poor of Mountsorrel. The land and cottage they bought in 1617 is now part of Charity Farm.

This was an agricultural community, with a population in 1861 of 196 in Thurnby and 60 in Bushby, and although the railway came in 1870, there was little new building until the turn of the century. However, wealthy industrialists began to be attracted and building has gone on ever since on both sides of the Uppingham Road.

The centre of village life is still in Main Street, Thurnby, with the church, school, and Memorial Hall, which is used by more than 20 different organisations. The post office and store is in the Square, Scouts and Guides have their own headquarters near and the village fete, which was revived several years ago, is held on the school field in the late summer.

Stoughton, called Stoctone in the Domesday Book, is about a mile across the valley south of Thurnby and Bushby, and some 500 yards east of the Roman Via Devana or Gartree Road. Its pleasant lands once belonged to Leicester Abbey, and near to the 600 year old church stands a 14th century cross, considered to be one of the county's most beautiful. In the church are many fine memorials and tombs of the Beaumont family, the lords of the manor, who lived at Stoughton Grange.

Early in the present century the whole estate was bought by the Co-operative Wholesale Society. One of the biggest farmers in Britain, the CWS have continued to farm with arable crops and large herds of Dairy Holstein cows.

The flat fields to the east of Stoughton were made into a Second World War aerodrome, used largely by the USAF. This is now a private airfield, run by the Leicester Aero Club and is the scene every August of a major air display, visited by Concorde, the Red Arrows and many other historic planes.

Tilton-on-the-Hill 🐾

Tilton-on-the-Hill is situated at the crossing of two ancient tracks which are believed to date from the Bronze Age. There are remains of Saxon stonework under parts of the foundations of the village inn.

The 'High Hill', said to be visible at times from the Lincoln coast, has three trees on the top. There seem to have always been trees planted at this spot and in medieval times the village was known as Tilton Three Trees. Locals call this place the Saxon burial tump and there is evidence that the Romans used the hill for a fort as there are steep ascents on all sides. A level surface on the top was encompassed by a ditch and low embankments, some of which are visible today.

The ancient church dominates the village and has been a landmark for the last 900 years. In recent times many a member of the Hunt when lost in the mist has been grateful for a sight of the church spire to find his way back.

The Digby family owned this land after the Norman Conquest until the 1600s. The most famous, or infamous, was Everard Digby, who was knighted by James I at Belvoir Castle in 1603. He was married for only three years when he was put to death for his part in the Gunpowder Plot.

The Nicholls family took over the patronage of the land in 1641 and until quite recently their descendants have lived in this area.

Four thousand years have passed since Tilton was on the track of early drovers following the Jurassic Way. A large proportion of today's travellers are families heading for a day's recreation at Rutland Water, little realising the age of the route they follow.

Tinwell 🐾

The tiny parish of Tinwell adjoins that of Stamford town on the northern bank of the river Welland and is on the far eastern boundary of Rutland.

There was a Saxon church here, belonging to Peterborough Abbey, but the Normans rebuilt on the same site. Only the lower part of the Norman tower remains, an unusual saddleback or gabled roof to the tower having been added about 1350, with further alterations made to the body of the church in the next century. After the Dissolution of the Monasteries, Henry VIII gave the church and manor of Tinwell to the Cecil family of nearby Burghley House, with whom links have been strong ever since.

The farms are occupied by tenants of the Cecil Estate Family Trust (following the death of the 6th Marquess of Exeter) and the only other

173

industry is at The Forge, where ornamental work is produced alongside works of traditional blacksmithing. The big door to the smithy is framed by a huge stone horseshoe, portraying the purpose for which it was built in 1848. The bakery has given way to a small village shop, next door to the one and only public house, and all front onto a miniscule village green. A mill by the river, making stoneground flour, had an unhappy history: a boiler explosion badly damaged the buildings and killed two men in 1887 and this was followed by a serious fire in 1894. The rebuilt mill was finally closed in 1914 and has now been converted to very attractive homes.

When the village school was closed it became the village hall, where the Youth Club meet and village functions are held, but the annual Fair and Feast, which used to be enjoyed on the Sunday after 1st November, ceased to be held at the beginning of the First World War.

A favourite tease was to ask newcomers if they had visited Tinwell Docks and Treacle Mines. The location of these mysteries is believed to be clay-filled hollows from which stone and iron ore had been dug on the Easton hillside and the loading docks from which the material had been carted away.

There used to be two toll gates in the village: that at the eastern end was pulled down about 1914 and the western one disappeared in the 1950s.

The older dwellings are of local limestone, with Collyweston slated roofs, but development since the First World War has added brick houses and doubled the population to a little more than 200. Apart from the few engaged in local farming, most villagers travel to work in Stamford or Peterborough.

Twycross

Twycross is a small village on the A444, midway between Nuneaton and Burton on Trent, with a population of approximately 250.

Twycross has over the years been closely linked to Gopsall Hall and was part of the Gopsall estate. Several houses and lanes were named after members of the Gopsall family. In 1920 the Gopsall estate was sold to Lord Waring. He then sold all of the estate except the Hall and parklands to the Crown Estates in 1927. The Hall and park were used by troops during the Second World War, and were purchased by the Crown afterwards. The Hall fell into disrepair and was demolished in 1950. The Crown have sold most of the cottages in the village but still own the farms.

In 1564 there were 28 houses in the village. The number has increased over the years to the present 120, consisting of a council estate, two private estates, the older cottages and six farms.

Charles Jennens, once lord of the manor, was a friend and patron of Handel and it is believed that he wrote parts of the *Messiah* while staying at Gopsall Hall. He also wrote the music to the hymn *Rejoice the Lord is King* there. The tune to it is called *Gopsall*.

Twycross House, in the centre of the village, was a well known hunting box of the Viscount Curzon until it was sold. It is now a private school.

St James the Great church was built of stone during the 13th century and is famous for its east window which contains perhaps the oldest stained glass in England, dating from about 1145. It came mostly from Sainte Chappelle in Paris and the Cathedral of St Denis north of Paris. It was purchased in France after the French Revolution. It came into the possession of George III and was given to Earl Howe of Gopsall by William IV.

The Church of England school was demolished in 1930 and the bricks were used to build the present village hall on the same site. The village has two successful cricket teams, who can often be seen during the summer playing on the cricket field in the centre of the village.

Twyford 🦌

Twyford was recorded in the Domesday Book as 'Tuivorde', for the obvious reason of its two fords over the brook. Up to around 1950 the village was purely agricultural and quite self-sufficient, having a baker, two butchers, a plumber, two shoemakers, a carpenter who was the undertaker, and a blacksmith. There were three provision shops, one incorporating the post office and two public houses. Now there are two shops (one with the post office) and one public house – The Saddle Inn.

There are two buildings of note in the village, St Andrew's church and the former village school. The church has a commanding site in the centre of the village. It is notable for a Corinthian capital carved by masons who then moved on to Oakham Castle, where an exact copy may be seen. The Twyford work was believed to be started in 1175. The church has also an unusual 13th century font.

Unfortunately the school has had to close and the building is now a private house. At the beginning of the century Mr William Boyes was the headmaster. He kept daily records which gave very precise details. Reasons for absence were varied, such as haymaking, harvesting, man-

175

gold pulling, potato picking, gleaning corn etc. Mr Boyes was highly respected and a bell was added in the church to his memory.

For transport a railway station called John O'Gaunt was half a mile from the village. It was a joint LNER and LMSR making Leicester, Grantham, Market Harborough and Nottingham visitable. It was a short journey to Melton Mowbray. This line was closed in the 1960s.

The brook is part of Twyford. The 'town bridge' of three stone arches, built in 1775, was where witches were ducked. Later, probably during the middle of the 19th century, the bridge was widened to take two lines of traffic, horses and carts. It is amazing that this same bridge carries present day very heavy traffic.

There is another bridge on the John O'Gaunt Road, and a footbridge in Stepping Lane. The village is subject to severe flooding, the roads through the village then being impassable to cars. However, due to work carried out during the last few years to clean out the brook downstream, the floods are less severe.

In the churchyard, Absalom Smith, King of the Gipsies was interred. He died in February 1826 aged 60 years, leaving a wife and 13 children. He was playing the fiddle in the Saddle Inn when taken ill. The family was in camp in Freizeland Lane, three-quarters of a mile from Twyford on the Queniborough Road. Mourners came long distances and were supposed to have stretched in two's from the Freizeland Lane to the church.

A local man, George Porter Riley, had a book of poems published in 1896. The most notable, if not the most profound, started 'Twyford Mill stands on the hill and if it's not gone it stands there still'. Well, it went around 1910. It stood on the right hand side of the road to Thorpe Satchville.

Ullesthorpe ✑

Ullesthorpe has one of Leicestershire's largest earthworks, and Leicestershire Museums archaeologists who surveyed the site, have found evidence of substantial fish farming in a series of ponds and a moat. It is thought the site probably dates from around 1300.

Years ago most of the residents earned their living working on the land, but the village in the early 20th century was self-sufficient in that it had a butcher, baker, cobbler, wheelwright, stockmaker, policeman, horsetrainer, blacksmith, carters, coal merchant, builder, doctor, milliner, brickworks, post office and general store.

Once Ullesthorpe was the home of the Midland's largest annual sheep sale, but today on the field where the sheep pens stood there are 70 homes and bungalows, and a school now stands where the actual market used to be. The majority of the inhabitants now travel out of the village to work.

The Court, once the home of Mr and Mrs Hugh Goodacre, who owned most of the land in and around Ullesthorpe was a fine country mansion. It was used as a VAD hospital during the First World War. It was then turned into flats, then used for storing grain, and now after much alteration is a thriving country golf club and restaurant.

A character who most local people remember is Miss Jenny Wren. She lived in Manor Cottages and worked on the railway during the Second World War. In the evenings she played the piano for the weekly 'tanner hop'. (This was a dance where you paid 6d to get in.) It is thought that she came to the village with the Edwards family, who were travelling players.

Unfortunately Ullesthorpe lost its station in 1963. Prior to this, grain was despatched from the station together with loads of timber from the woodyard at Claybrooke Magna, and in the later years, chickens from the poultry farm at Leire.

Ullesthorpe has a mill, although it has no sails. This was built by the farmers of the area, who all subscribed to it. Grain was stored in the granary in Mill Road, now converted into cottages.

Ullesthorpe is also reputed to be the home of Leicester cheese. It is believed that Mr Tomlinson made the cheese first in Ashby Parva, later moving to Ullesthorpe.

Walcote 🌿

The Anglo-Saxon village of Walcote, in the parish of Misterton, is a village of some 400 inhabitants. It lies one and a half miles east of Lutterworth and eleven miles west from Market Harborough on the A427 road.

Two centuries ago Walcote had four public houses; The Bull's Head, The Red Lion, The Crown (now The Tavern) and The Black Horse. Only the last two remain.

Along with the public houses a number of the older houses have been demolished and replaced by small modern starter homes and some larger ones. Still standing are several Victorian houses and also one or two cottages of the 16th century which have been attractively renovated and modernised. The character of Walcote, like villages throughout the country, has changed dramatically over the centuries. Where in times past most of the menfolk were labourers on the adjoining farms the village was well served by a smithy, bakery, shop, school and post office, today it is a dormitary village for commuters.

Development in Walcote has been limited and the small community has been unable to adequately support a post office, shop or school. The school was closed in 1984 owing to the lack of children of primary school age.

St Leonard's church, which serves the parish of Walcote and Misterton, is said to have been erected circa 1335. An unusual feature is the priest's room situated above the porch. A centuries old yew tree, positioned at the entrance to the church, sweeps over the gateway to form an arch and a most picturesque entrance to the churchyard.

The church was built to serve the parish of Misterton, which in the 14th century comprised the villages of Walcote, Poultney and Misterton. The last two have disappeared over the centuries and only Walcote remains, retaining access via an ancient footpath just less than one mile from the village. The church is also accessible via a modern road. As well as the Anglican church at Misterton there were two chapels located in the village. One, called the Mission Room, is disused and the other, in Chapel Lane, has been turned into a house.

In the reign of James I, Misterton rabbits were preferred 'for their goodness and delicate flavour before all others which were taken there' and were sent regularly to the London Court.

Towards the end of 1910 the inhabitants were shocked by a brutal murder – a stranger had been seen loitering in the village, and later that day the body of an old lady, Mrs Harris, was found strangled in her cottage behind the Black Horse. Her hoard of threepenny pieces was missing. Apparently the stranger made his way to an hotel in Rugby, where he paid his bill in threepenny pieces. Suspicious, the hotelier informed the police. The man, named Palmer, was arrested, found guilty and hanged at Leicester jail on 24th January 1911. This macabre affair gained the title of 'The Threepenny Bit Murder'.

Walton on the Wolds ❧

Walton on the Wolds is a small, quiet village four miles from Loughborough. The name is derived from the Saxon 'Waletone', mentioned in the Domesday survey.

It has always been a predominantly farming community and although less people work on the land today there are still twelve working farms. Some are situated away from the village since the Enclosure Acts of 1792 and 1796 re-allocated the ownership of the three great fields – Bybarrow, Cockling Croft Field and Long Sike Field.

This is a conservation area but some new houses have been built. Walton's oldest building is the black and white timber-framed structure of more than 600 years old known as Kingscote, from the legend that Richard III sheltered here on the night before the Battle of Bosworth. Opposite stands the Old Manor, a brick and timber house built in 1560 with 1845 additions.

Nearby is the Anchor Inn with a bar called Hobart's Cabin, both so named after Augustus Charles Hobart-Hampden, later known as Hobart Pasha. Born at the rectory in 1822, his father was the 6th Earl of Buckingham, the then rector. He joined the Royal Navy, and became a blockade runner for the forces of the South in the American Civil War. In 1867 he was struck off the Naval List for becoming a naval adviser to the Turks and became Admiral of the Ottoman Fleet. Later he was reinstated with the rank of Rear Admiral.

This area is in the heart of the Quorn Hunt country and in the season the Hunt meets at the inn and on the green making a very picturesque scene.

The blacksmith's shop where Thomas Gambel, blacksmith in 1704, was also a clockmaker has disappeared. An example of his brass-faced clocks is in Newarke Houses Museum, Leicester. The school is closed, only living on in the names School Hill and School House. The only shop, the post office, is run in a private house.

Centuries ago there stood a fine manor house, the home of the Mallory family to the south of the church. This was destroyed during the Civil War. The name is still used for the present building near the site, and was occupied by the Masons for many years.

The original Gothic church of St Bartholomew was erected in 1220. According to Nichols this church was one of the most beautiful in the county. This building, becoming ruinous, was demolished and rebuilt in 1739 in brick and stone and re-named St Mary's.

Another incumbent of 48 years from 1894 to 1942, the Rev Montague Bertie Bird, had some strange hobbies, the most famous being trick photography in which he produced a photograph of himself flying over the church. He also composed long narrative poetry.

Welham 🦢

The small village of Welham, which has a population of about 36, lies on the Leicestershire side of the river Welland about four miles north-east of Market Harborough. The first written reference to the village is in the Domesday Book, when it was called 'Weleham'. The first mention of the church is in 1098, recording the presence of a priest in the village. It is thought, however, that the village is Saxon in origin.

When the Edwards family, from Kibworth and ancestors of the Earl of Gainsborough, acquired the estate in 1717, a new village was built in its present form, on the opposite side of the road to the old settlement. Francis Edwards also constructed a new hall to the north of the village, of which only the garden walls and main gates remain. Besides rebuilding the village and the 'Old Red Lion', Edwards planned a turnpike road through Welham, which would run from Leicester to London. His scheme was not accepted and the turnpike went through Market Harborough, along what is now the A6.

Francis Edwards did not neglect the church in Welham. He rebuilt part of the nave walls. The chancel was demolished and a new pointed window with no tracery replaced the chancel arch. It was probably at this time that a porch was built on the south side of the church. The date of this work was 1720. Francis Edwards died in 1728 and in his memory his only daughter, Mary Edwards, erected the monument now housed in the mausoleum. The monument originally stood outside in the churchyard to the east of the church. It did not weather well so in 1809 the Edwards family ordered the monument to be dismantled. It was taken to Stamford to be cleaned and repaired by Mr Sparrow, a marble mason. He was also instructed to build a mausoleum to house the monument. It was poorly constructed and was soon in a state of disrepair. In fact to this day the whole addition to the church at that time is a continual worry to the churchwardens, forever needing attention and repair.

Welham has always been subject to flooding from the Welland. The most disastrous flood of 1880 swept away the road bridge. This was replaced the next year by the present bridge. Since the Anglian Water Authority completed major work on cleaning the river, flooding has not recurred.

The village has not changed much over the centuries. The only addition has been four council houses and a private house. The Old Red Lion has been extended to give a function room and this is very popular. There is only one farm now in the village, the land having been amalgamated to form one unit. The type of farming has not changed, though, with the rich Welland valley pasture still being used to fatten cattle and sheep.

Whetstone

Engulfed by suburban Leicester, and still subject to housing developments, the old village of Whetstone lies five miles south-west of the city of Leicester.

The 1086 Domesday Book records Whetstone as having 24 peasants, 11 villeins, one man at arms and a windmill. For the next eight centuries the village lived quietly following agricultural pursuits, with the 18th century addition of some framework knitting.

The parish church of St Peter, built around 1335 contains some interesting carvings. One, immediately over the east window shows the three faces of the Trinity in one. The capital of a supporting pillar of the chancel arch was evidently carved by a mason with a wicked sense of humour. A face looking at the congregation has its tongue out. Facing the altar the same carving has a hand superimposed over the tongue. Outside can be seen mass dials and a consecration cross.

There do not appear to have been any large houses built until the arrival of the Hind family, who quarried the famous 'Swithland' slate. One member built a house just south of the Great Central Railway. This house is remembered by the 'Hinds Crossing', a foot crossing on the nearby Leicester to Birmingham railway. Another Hind purchased a large estate south of the village and built a spacious house with farm buildings (now a residential home for the elderly). Slate is much in evidence on this estate, including what is reputed to be the largest block of slate ever quarried. The Pastures then passed into the ownership of the Herbert family who still farm the estate.

The years immediately before the end of the Second World War saw the arrival of a new industry, aero engine development. This was Mr (later 'Sir') Frank Whittle with his pioneering work on the jet engine. The present GEC complex is the successor to that enterprise.

Roads on new housing estates commemorate various village notables – Buxton Close, for example, after Joseph Buxton, a candlemaker and local benefactor. He had trees planted by the village brook and in 1907 gave two bells to the village church.

The names of incumbents from 1867, when Whetstone became a separate parish, are remembered as street names on the Vicarage housing estate.

Whissendine

Years ago the villagers worked on the land or in service for the gentry who lived in their 'hunting boxes' during the winter season. Few inhabitants work in the village now. Most of those living on the new estates are professional people.

There are two public houses known as the 'Top' and the 'Bottom': the Three Horseshoes and the White Lion respectively. Next door to the latter is the Village Memorial Hall, built in 1937 to commemorate George V.

Forryans, the butchers, make their own sausages, haslet and pies, and theirs is the only shop apart from the Post Office Stores. Underwood's West End garage is next to the old navvies yard, which was built in 1844 by the railway company.

The Sherrards of Stapleford owned the village until 1867. In 1859, on the insistence of his wife, who objected to his mistress living so close, Lord Harborough had the home of Eliza Temple of Stowe removed from the grounds of Stapleford Park and rebuilt on a smaller scale in Whissendine. An original chimney can still be seen at Stapleford. The house, in Stapleford Road, was renamed Harborough Cottage in 1919.

The mill having six floors is the second tallest in the country. It was constructed of stone from the walls of Stapleford Park, which Lord Harborough demolished because 'they kept in the foxes'. Whissendine station was built two miles away as Lord Harborough refused permission for the line to cross his land. He had shares in the competing canal company!

The Red House in the Nook was once Whissendine Brewery. Originally trading as Green and Acker, it closed in 1893 and the top storey was removed.

St Andrew's church, described as a 'village cathedral' by the Bishop of Peterborough on a walking pilgrimage, was built by Joan, Princess of Wales, in memory of her husband, the Black Prince.

At the annual parish meeting in March, the custom of 'Letting the Banks' takes place. The Banks is an area of pasture which is let by the pin and candle method. A candle is lit, a pin inserted near the top, and the last person to bid as the pin drops out is entitled to graze sheep or horses on the land for the next year.

Wigston Magna 🪶

Wigston Magna was previously known as Wigston Two Steeples, being distinguished for centuries by two churches, each with its own steeple. The more stately of these churches is All Saints, six centuries old. The other church with its 14th century steeple is dedicated to St Wistan, later known as St Wolstan, the 11th century Bishop of Worcester, who had a tireless devotion to the lowly.

Wigston may claim to have been an important place in Saxon days, for many ornaments have been unearthed locally, along with Saxon horse trappings. Originally a 'ring fenced' village, four roads lined with cottages enclosed an area of about 40 acres, being ringed round by a fence as a protection from the surrounding forest.

In the early 1700s, with the advent of the knitting frames, the first signs of industry other than agriculture began to appear in Wigston. There followed the opening of the Grand Union Canal in 1798, and in 1840 the Leicester to Rugby railway line was opened. Prior to 1939, the principal local industries were hosiery and boots and shoes, but there are now many more newly established industries including electrical and general engineering, printing, plastics, musical instrument manufacture and ancillary industries to the footwear trade. Since 1946, new industrial estates have risen amongst the residential developments, providing employment within easy reach of their homes for the local inhabitants.

On 4th February 1946, a Polish Lancaster Bomber on a training flight was struck by lightning over South Wigston and crashed into the field between Central Avenue and Aylestone Lane, in Wigston Magna. This is now the site of the Lancaster Bell school building and community wing, 'Bell' being a link with the old Bell Street school. The Polish Air Force Association have placed a memorial plaque in the community wing, and every year a short service is held by them in both Polish and English.

Willoughby Waterleys 🪶

Willoughby Waterleys is a small village some eight miles due south of Leicester. It is mentioned in the Domesday Book but it has never been large or of great importance. The manorial rights have moved from family to family and certainly in the Middle Ages were a pawn in the many arguments between Crown and Barons. Its name comes from the many springs that lie near the surface and the two rivulets that run through the parish.

183

It is a single street with two cul-de-sacs leading off. The church dates from Norman times and until 1972 there was a Primitive Methodist chapel. The chapel was built in 1877 to replace a thatched building that had been previously used. There was a rumour that 'something was behind the corner stone' and on its conversion from chapel to private property a bottle was found there, containing a copy of a Methodist magazine of 1877. Before replacing the corner stone a new bottle containing a copy of the latest *Leicester Mercury* together with a letter was placed where the original bottle had been.

Willoughby grew in the 18th century. The Limes, a lovely Queen Anne farmhouse, was built in 1702 and Old Hall (thought to have been built soon after 1600) was enlarged and modified by Richard Gamble – the date can be seen in blue bricks on the south gable. These two houses are connected by ghost lore, there being a story of the daughter of the Limes falling in love with her piano tutor who lived at Old Hall. But her brother stopped her elopement and killed the young man. The daughter, to show her distress, then married a labourer and lived in Thurmaston.

Manor Farm, Willoughby Waterleys

During the early part of the 20th century Willoughby had a number of small hosiery factories, the largest being at the north end of the village where eight people were employed working 'Griswolds'. It was the job of the school children to 'wind on' in their lunch hour and again after school.

In the latter half of the 19th century Willoughby had three shops, a beerhouse, fruiterer, dressmaker, carpenter, three hosiery factories, a boot and shoe factory, a wheelwright and blacksmith. The main industry throughout the ages has been agriculture. Eleven farms/graziers are mentioned in the latter half of the 19th century, today the same number are worked but with the help of modern methods and machinery employ only one man (the owner) or sometimes two. The majority of the residents now go out of the village for work.

Wing

The village of Wing is situated on the brow of a hill overlooking the river Chater and the Oakham to Norwich railway line in the valley.

Wing has a good variety of old and interesting buildings, many of them built in the 17th century in local Clipsham stone and roofed in Colly-weston slate or thatch. There are several large houses with interesting histories. The Old Hall in the centre of the village and the newer Wing Hall on the outskirts are testimony to the wealth that has been in the village. Both were occupied by the Worrall family, who remain substantial landowners. Wing Grange, now owned by the Langley Trust, became famous in the early 20th century as the home of the remarkable Miss Brocklebank. She was a famous horsewoman who drove her tandem pair *Optimist* and *Illumination* to win the Championship of Dublin Show in 1912, 1913 and again in 1919. They were also four times Champions of the Royal Show. Miss Brocklebank also established a noted herd of beef shorthorns called the 'Wing herd'.

Farming has always been the centre of Wing life but this is changing rapidly. There is only one full time farm labourer living in the village now and the recent conversion of farm buildings into an 'Antiques Centre' and workshop unit show the change that is taking place. Tourism and the influence of Rutland Water can be seen all around; Leicester is only half an hour away by car. The chairmakers, fellmongers and wheelwrights of the past have been replaced by professional people. Even the allotment gardens, fully used during the depression of the 1930s, are less popular now.

185

The village pubs, the King's Arms and the Cuckoo, are important meeting places in the village. There is a legend that Wing villagers once attempted to fence in the cuckoo so that they could enjoy spring the whole year through. Not surprisingly Wing folk were called 'Wing Fools'.

However, one woman in the early 19th century became famous as the 'Wise Woman of Wing'. Amelia Woodcock was a herbalist, and her medicines were sold around the district by a man riding on a donkey as well as from her cottage. Her house no longer exists but 'City Yard' is a reminder of the time when gentry and city folk visited the wise woman. She died about 1850 but her remedies were still for sale in Boots the chemist in Uppingham right up until the 1950s.

One of the main tourist attractions is 'Wing Maze'. The maze, situated on the edge of the village is reputed to be medieval. It is cut out of turf and not something to get lost in. There is a tradition that penitents were made to crawl around the maze and say prayers at certain points. Perhaps it was considered to be of some supernatural or holy significance in earlier times and it is certainly linked to the knot gardens of the great English houses and the labyrinths of Greek mythology. By the 19th century the maze seems to have lost some of its magic, for the Leicester and Rutland Directory of 1846 talks of: 'An ancient Maze, in which the rustics run at the parish feast'.

Witherley 🐚

Watery Witherley would be a very good description of the pleasant village that lies in the south-west corner of Leicestershire, although since the improvements in the flow of the river Anker, which divides it from Warwickshire on its southern side, the floods are not as spectacular as they used to be.

There has been a church on the site since earliest times and it became a parish church in 1173. For at least 500 years the lofty spire of the present 14th century building has been a landmark in the countryside around. After being destroyed by lightning in 1924, it was shortened when rebuilt but is still nearly 160 feet high. Plaques within the church record ancient charities, one of which, dated 19th February 1689, gave five shillings worth of bread to the poor on Ascension Day. Now subsidised, the schoolchildren are given buns on this day.

The well known Atherstone Hunt has its stables and kennels at Witherley. Founded by 'the Squire', George Osbaldeston, and Hugo

Meynell who defined its boundaries, the Hunt was the subject of a book by Siegried Sassoon – *The Memoirs of a Foxhunting Man*.

Witherley can claim to be associated with the start of the Shrove Tuesday football game in Atherstone. The legend is that King John put up a bag of gold as a stake in a football match between the lads of Leicestershire and Warwickshire. It is believed this was in fact a match between Witherley and Atherstone, which Atherstone won. A golden penny is still thrown to the crowds at the start of the game.

The oldest surviving house is the 16th century, half-timbered black and white yeoman's house in Mythe Lane.

The imposing Hall, mainly Victorian mock Tudor, has a ballroom wing, built in 1930 by the Chamberlayne family who dominated the village in Hall and rectory for many years. There is an enormous vaulted ice house submerged in the grounds on the south side of the house. Used for housing prisoners during the Second World War, the house has now been beautifully restored by the present owners.

Next to the 18th century inn, The Blue Lion, are two cottages with a large terracotta plaque commemorating the Diamond Jubilee of Queen Victoria.

The village before the Second World War must have been almost self-supporting for there was a smithy, bakery, slaughterhouse, mill, post office and a shop. A tremendous change has taken place since the 1960s. Old cottages have been knocked down or modernised. There are now no farms within the village, the land has been taken for building and the stabling turned into mews cottages. It is a very prosperous area, with beautiful houses and gardens belonging to professional and business people.

Woodhouse & Woodhouse Eaves

The picturesque village of Woodhouse Eaves lies on the northern edge of scenic Charnwood Forest and attracts visitors from near and far. It is a village of many pretty stone cottages, roofed in the coveted Swithland slate. The local slate and stone quarries, brickyards and kilns, now disused, employed many of the villagers whose families originally occupied these cottages. It is known that the quarries were worked in Roman times.

In the early part of this century, there was a brickyard and kiln on the land which is now known as Hill Rise. This kiln made the bricks for Beaumanor Hall and was approached by Post Office Drive. Also about this time, there were stockingers' houses at 1 Mill Road and 47 Maple-well Road. The Griswold machines (stockinger's machines) were worked by gas engine and about six local girls used them.

What is now known as 1 Victoria Road was originally called Liberty Hall and was built by Maurice Levy, the Liberal Agent. The balcony was used by him to address the villagers at election time. There was a little grocery shop underneath and later the whole building was bought by Sir Arthur Wheeler and loaned as a village club.

The blacksmith's shop was opposite Ye Olde Bulls Head, while in Beacon Road the undertakers and coachmakers carried on their business. Fountain Cottage was originally the Fountain Cafe and the village 'hops' were held in a tin shed at the rear – dancing classes were given to the music of Harry Lester's Hayseeds!

Standing on a hill overlooking the centre of the village is the spendid church of St Paul, designed in 1837 by W. Railton. The church was built here as a result of the forest enclosures. Fronting the Main Street are the Baptist and Methodist churches, the Baptist church being attractively modernised in 1981.

Nearby Woodhouse, sometimes known as Old Woodhouse, is a much smaller village, charmingly winding its way from the gates of Beaumanor Hall to the church of St Mary in the Elms, a very old foundation. Beaumanor Hall, home of the Herrick family for many generations, is now owned by Leicestershire County Council.

On the edge of the two villages stands Beacon Hill, a Bronze Age settlement. As its name implies, it was the site for a warning beacon. Up until relatively recent times, permits were needed to get on to Hanging Stone and the Beacon, but they were open to the public on Bank Holiday Mondays, when extra police were brought in to control the crowds. Many of the cottages sold refreshments and jugs of tea.

The Brand is the home of the former Lord Lieutenant of Leicestershire, Col Sir Andrew Martin, KCVO, OBE, LLD, JP, whose family have given long service to the county. In the lovely gardens and grounds are some of the old slate quarries and in this area was the old branding station for stock.

Worthington

Worthington is a small village between Ashby-de-la-Zouch and Coal-ville. There are two pubs, one chapel, one church, a post office shop and an excellent school. The chapel is square and whitewashed, the church of St Matthew is ancient stone and beautiful.

The octagonal Round House is an old lock-up and is featured on the bright red sweatshirts which form part of the new school uniform. There are several listed buildings and some protected trees. Cloud Wood, a greatly undervalued site of special scientific interest lies on the edge of a quarry.

Development, from the time of the council estate built in the 1950s, has brought new life to the village. The school is thriving and there are more 'regulars' in the pub, and even in the church! From 1991 the A42 will run by the village and will bring more changes.

Wymondham & Edmondthorpe

The villages of Edmondthorpe and Wymondham are situated on the border of Lincolnshire.

Roman occupation sites have been discovered; an extensive villa site in Wymondham in 1796 and a possibly even larger site at Edmondthorpe in 1798 when a hoard of coins was uncovered during the excavation of a large cutting for the Oakham to Melton canal. A third Roman occupation site exists opposite the Wymondham windmill.

The Berkeleys of Berkeley Castle in Gloucestershire inherited the Manor estate by marriage. They trained their local militia in the butts off what is now Butt Lane. Sir John Berkeley raised a local contingent who excelled themselves at the battle of Crecy in 1346 and the lord of the manor was granted a free warren in the parish by the King in recognition of the excellence of the Wymondham bowmen. This area of land is still called big and little Cunery, a long, rolling hill to the south of the village. Sir Henry Berkeley sold the estate to Sir John Sedley in 1635. Sir John left £400 in his will for the education of the children of Wymondham. A trust fund formed by his widow still continues and generates considerable income to support educational facilities in the village.

The opening of the Melton to Oakham canal in 1803 had considerable impact on village life, especially in Edmondthorpe where the canal ran the whole length of the estate. Three locks, a lock-keeper's cottage and public house existed solely to support the canal boatmen and the necessary maintenance workers. All have disappeared, demolished shortly after the canal closed in 1847.

Wymondham was noted as one of the major manufacturing areas for Stilton cheese. This cream cheese was manufactured by the Paulet family in Wymondham and transported to the Bell Inn at Stilton on the Great North Road. From a farmyard product it developed into a major manufacturing industry, though it declined after the First World War. Cheese is no longer made in the factory that still stands in the village, only a well-known brand of a dried herb product.

A sporting event of international importance, albeit illegal, took place in the parish of Wymondham on 28th September 1811 – the first defence of the heavyweight championship of the world between the challenger, the American negro Tom Molyneux, and the holder, Tom Cribb of London. These two prize-fighters fought eleven rounds on a staged ring in a stubble field near Thistleton Gap, lasting 19 minutes ten seconds before a crowd of approximately 20,000 people. The combined stake money amounted to about £50,000. Tom Cribb was declared the winner when the challenger could not stand for any further punishment.

Local superstition surrounds the Smith monument in Edmondthorpe church. Sir Roger Smith, lord of the manor of Edmondthorpe, died in 1655. An alabaster tomb was erected over his grave with effigies of his two wives. One, that of Lady Ann Smith, has a red stain on the wrist. She was considered to be a witch who could turn herself into a cat. During her lifetime, a white cat, who was a considerable thief, was resident in the Hall. One morning the butler caught the cat in the kitchen and attempted to kill it with a cleaver. The cat was wounded in the paw. Dripping blood, it fled out of the window never to be seen again. That day Lady Ann appeared with a bandaged wrist. When the bandages were eventually removed a red scar was clearly visible on her wrist. This red mark appears on her effigy in Edmondthorpe church and is said to 'bleed' under certain circumstances. The stain made by the cat's blood etched into the flagstones on the kitchen floor for centuries and it was impossible to remove it, even with repeated scrubbing. Finally, Lady Yarborough had the offending stones removed in 1920. These were on display in Gollings Workshop in Wymondham for a number of years.

In the centre of the small village of Edmondthorpe stands the ruins of Edmondthorpe Hall, built by the Smith family and extensively altered and renovated by the Pochin family of Barkby, the present estate owners.

The Hall, then being used as a prisoner of war camp, was destroyed by fire in 1943. The blaze lit up the night sky. The flames, reaching up to the moon, could be clearly seen from the neighbouring village of Wymondham. Even this disaster was attributed to the Smiths. The reincarnation of Lady Ann Smith – the white cat – was always being seen by soldiers and prisoners alike. The fire is said to have been started by the cook throwing a rolling pin at the cat, upsetting a candle into a pan of fat, so starting the disastrous fire – so legends begin!

Index

191